HOW DID THE HARAPPANS SAY HELLO?

Anu Kumar now lives in Maryland, US, having already lived in and travelled to several places. Her historical fiction includes the Atisa series. Her non-fiction includes *In the Country of Gold-digging Ants*. She also writes for older readers; her recent books in this category are *It Takes a Murder* and *Inspector Angre and the Pizza Delivery Boy*.

Kavita Singh Kale has been illustrating and writing for children's books, music videos and short films for over a decade now. She has a BFA in painting from New Delhi and a PG degree in Animation from the National Institute of Design, Ahmedabad.

Other books in the series

What if the Earth Stopped Spinning?
And 24 Other Mysteries of Science

Do Tigers Drink Blood?
And 13 Other Mysteries of Nature

HOW DID THE HARAPPANS SAY HELLO?

AND 16 OTHER MYSTERIES OF HISTORY

Anu Kumar

Illustrated by
Kavita Singh Kale

RED TURTLE
RUPA

Published in Red Turtle by
Rupa Publications India Pvt. Ltd 2014
7/16, Ansari Road, Daryaganj
New Delhi 110002

Sales centres:
Allahabad Bengaluru Chennai
Hyderabad Jaipur Kathmandu
Kolkata Mumbai

ISBN: 978-81-291-3131-7

First impression 2014

10 9 8 7 6 5 4 3 2 1

Printed at Shree Maitrey Printech Pvt. Ltd., Noida

For all students of history, present and future, in the certainty that history is fun and does much for our understanding and empathy

CONTENTS

HOW DID THE HARAPPANS SAY HELLO?

HOW DID WE DISCOVER HARAPPA?

It was the year 1826, when a soldier who had deserted the British army found himself in Sindh (which is now in northwest Pakistan). He stopped by the banks of the river Indus, where he noticed the low hills and mounds that surrounded the area. What was strange was that these mounds weren't continuous; they had stretches of barren ground in between.

The soldier's name was James Lewis and he wasn't particularly good at history. But still all this made him curious. Maybe he saw some artefacts (you know, those things of historical interest you find in museums) lying around, which made him think. He became convinced this was the site where Alexander the Great had fought his great battle with Porus more than 1800 years ago (yes, the same one you read about in your history textbook in class).

No one around seemed to know much about the place, although for centuries this area had stood in the pathway of tribes and groups that wandered by. (The people of these tribes survived by moving up to the colder highlands during summer, and coming down once again in the winter when the snow made it too cold for them to live in the mountains.)

So anyway, James Lewis penned his own accounts of his travels. He wrote these books using the pen name Charles Mason, and one of these was even composed in verse, and had Lewis's own illustrations: he was a remarkably talented soldier!

However, the mystery about this site that Lewis had chanced on was nowhere near solved. Soon after Lewis, an East India Company official, Alexander Burnes, also visited it. He had worked closely with scholars like James Prinsep who were interested in old inscriptions that helped them understand India's past (because, of course, the British ruled India then, and they wanted to know as much as possible about the country they were ruling). Then in 1850s, Alexander Cunningham, a British army engineer and archaeology enthusiast, conducted excavations in the area James Lewis had stumbled upon. As the details emerged, it was a surprise how long this huge secret had remained buried...

SO WHAT DID THEY FIND?

As part of his excavations, Cunningham found some stone tools and ancient pottery. Hmm, you ask, what's so special about a bunch of old stuff? Oh, but wait, there's more! He also found a seal (you know, those things people in ancient times used to close letters and things, back before they had email, poor things). The seal

Cunningham: The archaeologist whose work turned stories into history

showed a bull without a hump. Cunningham noticed that there was some strange writing on it. He thought that maybe it was a foreign seal, which had come from outside India, through trade. But once excavations began to be conducted systematically, more seals were found.

Most of them were rectangular, and some were really quite tiny, and they all had strange animals engraved on them. On some, there was a unicorn, on others, there were elephants, buffaloes, and a type of deer called chinkara. Some seals even showed the tiger and the gharial (a kind of crocodile) as well as the dolphin that once was common in the Ganga.

The seals were made of soapstone, and baked with a kind of printmaking technique called 'intaglio', so that the patterns on the seals looked like stencil creations (yes, like the ones you do in Arts and Craft class).

BUT WAIT, WHAT DID THESE SEALS MEAN?

So that's the mystery. NO ONE KNOWS! The writing on the top of the seals that Cunningham first discovered was in a script that was also found on other inscriptions and tablets found in the area. And because it has never been deciphered, the mystery surrounding these sites still remains unsolved.

WHAT HAPPENED NEXT?

In the twentieth century, more and more sites began to be excavated, first along the river Indus and then over a wider area. But there was a slight problem. You see, the site was declared a protected area only after several decades after it was found. So all through the mid nineteenth century, engineers and other railway workers dug out the ancient remains since a railway line was being built from Lahore to Multan (both of which are now in Pakistan). And that wasn't all: the people living in the modern town of Harappa (also in Pakistan), not too far away from the ancient site, had probably helped themselves to the old bricks and other artefacts from the remains for generations, to use to build their own houses. So, of course, a lot of precious clues to the mystery were lost in the process.

Around 1920 regular excavation work formally began. Daya Ram Sahni of the Archaeological Survey of India oversaw the excavations near Harappa and in 1921, Rakhaldas Banerji started excavating the archaeological site of Mohenjo-daro (in Sindh, Pakistan).

BURIED CITIES AND THEIR SECRETS

So what did they find this time, you ask? Well, entire *cities*. Yes, you read that right. Remember the artefacts that were discovered by Cunningham and his team? Well, it seemed that was just the tip of the iceberg. Further digging revealed entire cities which had been lying in secret under the soil!

WHY IS IT CALLED THE HARAPPAN CIVILIZATION?

THESE CITIES WERE UNLIKE ANY THAT HAD BEEN DISCOVERED BEFORE. THEY WERE WELL PLANNED, WITH MUD-BRICK HOUSES, STREETS AT RIGHT ANGLES, GRANARIES AND EVEN A DRAINAGE SYSTEM. ALSO NO CITY WAS QUITE LIKE ANOTHER: THERE WAS A DOCKYARD IN LOTHAL IN GUJARAT, A CITADEL HIGH OVER THE CITY IN MOHENJO-DARO, A GREAT GRANARY IN HARAPPA. THE OTHER CITIES CAME TO BE IDENTIFIED ON THE BASIS OF THE KEY FEATURES THAT WERE FOUND AT HARAPPA, ONE OF THE EARLIEST SITES DISCOVERED. AND SO THE ENTIRE CIVILIZATION IS NOW CALLED THE HARAPPAN CIVILIZATION.

It was also discovered that the civilization spread much beyond what was believed originally. Not only were there cities and villages along the river Indus but also over a large region covering Pakistan, northwest and north India. The civilization spread over a vast area: 300,000 square miles and lasted for at least three millennia (yes, that's *three thousand years!*). Till date, more than 1,022 sites have been found, and only 97 have been fully excavated in India and Pakistan.

So how does this affect history as we know it?

Well, tremendously! The discovery of Harappa pushes back the history of our subcontinent by more than 2,500 years. Before this, the history of South Asia was believed to have begun with the sacred texts called the Vedas.

Rig Veda, the first of the four Vedas, was composed somewhere around the mid second century BCE, i.e. 1,500 BCE. Before the discovery of Harappa, history was derived mostly from written sources like the Vedas. But the Harappan sites proved that archaeology could do its own bit in revealing the mysteries of the past.

The Harappan sites were all dated using the scientific radiocarbon dating method; before this it was dated by placing it in context of the Mesopotamian Civilization (the ancient Greek civilization built on the banks of the Tigris-Euphrates rivers) that was contemporary to it.

There appeared to be at least three phases in the history of the Harappan Civilization: early Harappan, mature Harappan and late Harappan. The urban phase however was restricted to between 2,600-2,000 BCE.

So who were the Harappans exactly?

Since we still don't know how to read their script, much of what we know about Harappa is still shrouded in mystery. And since we can't be certain of anything, there are a LOT of different theories floating around about who the Harappans really were. Scholars and archaeologists, much like you and your sibling, can never seem to agree on *anything*!

Some scholars think that the Harappans were originally people from Sumer (South Mesopotamia, now Iraq) who migrated here. Others trace them to the farming communities who lived in

Baluchistan in the seventh millennium BCE. And there are several other theories about who the Harappans really were and where they came from, but the bottom-line is: We can never really be sure.

WHAT ABOUT THE MYSTERIOUS HARAPPAN LANGUAGE?

Ah, that's the greatest mystery of them all! Let's see what we do know about the writing of the Harappans:

So first, what is clear from the writing as it appears on seals and tablets is that there are 400-445 basic signs and the script is 'logo-syllabic' (which means that each symbol stands for a word or syllable). The writing appears to contain a lot of anthropomorphic signs, which is a fancy word for animals dressed up as humans. A common script appears to have been in use all over the Harappan cities, which means that some kind of cultural exchange happened between cities in the civilization.

Most of the inscriptions found on the seals are very short, with an average of five signs. The longest one has 26 signs.

THE DHOLAVIRA SIGNBOARD

THE DHOLAVIRA SIGNBOARD IS A DISCOVERY MADE IN THE ARCHAEOLOGICAL SITE OF DHOLAVIRA. THE HARAPPANS HAD ARRANGED TEN SYMBOLS ON A LARGE WOODEN BOARD TO INDICATE THAT IT WAS SOME KIND OF SIGN. AT SOME POINT, THIS SIGNBOARD FELL DOWN, AND THE WOOD DECAYED (BECAUSE, YOU KNOW, IT'S REALLY, REALLY OLD), BUT THE SYMBOLS REMAINED. NO ONE KNOWS WHAT THEY MEAN, OF COURSE, BUT IT'S IMPORTANT BECAUSE THIS INSCRIPTION IS ONE OF THE BIGGEST EVER FOUND IN THE HARAPPAN SCRIPT. IT'S ALSO AN EXAMPLE OF HOW, LIKE US, HARAPPANS USED GIANT SIGNS TO ANNOUNCE PUBLIC EVENTS (MAYBE THIS WAS A GIANT BILLBOARD!) AND ALSO POINTS TO THE FACT THAT MOST OF THE PEOPLE IN THE CITIES MUST HAVE KNOWN HOW TO READ.

The clay tablets found in and around the sites were perhaps used by merchants to validate their transactions or authenticate goods, much like the receipts we get nowadays for buying anything at a supermarket. What is also interesting is that the seals found at the Harappan sites are all worn on the edges and not on the inside. So they might have had other uses: like being used as tokens to exchange goods. They might have also been used as amulets or identity markers.

The Harappan script virtually disappeared by 1,700 BCE, and this coincides with the end of the urban phase of the civilization. Historians say that this probably means there was a close connection between writing and city life, and that with the end of the urban phase of the civilization, the writing itself also vanished.

DECODING THE SCRIPT: AN INDIAN DA VINCI CODE

So why hasn't the script been decoded yet? Surely there are so many language experts and people like that who can do this kind of stuff, right?

Well technically, yes. But the problem is, like theories on where the Harappans came from, no one can agree on how the script is supposed to be decoded.

Some believe it moves right to left. This is because in inscriptions, the letters are cramped on the left side where space has clearly run out. (Like how, when you're writing a heading for your essay, you start from the middle and can't fit everything into one line!)

Some archaeologists have found parallels with the script found in Mesopotamia, called the cuneiform script, which are wedge-shaped marks cut into stone. Many others have suggested that there's a link between the Harappan signs and the strange signs that look like 'bird-men' found several thousand miles away in the Pacific Ocean on Easter Island. (Look it up on Google, they're a little creepy!)

Some other scholars have suggested that the language of

the Harappan civilization belongs to the Dravidian family, that is the group of languages spoken in South India. Others have said that the Harappan script actually belongs to the Indo-Aryan family of languages, the branch from which languages like Sanskrit and Persian evolved.

SO HOW WILL WE EVER SOLVE THE MYSTERY?

Well, that's the big question.

When Egyptian hieroglyphs were discovered, the language remained a mystery for several years till the discovery of the Rosetta Stone, that was discovered in 1799 when Napoleon's French army invaded Egypt. The Rosetta Stone is basically a tablet engraved with text written in three different scripts: Ancient Egyptian, an ancient Demotic script and in Ancient Greek. Since the text was essentially the same, historians could figure out how Ancient Egyptian worked by comparing it with the other two scripts.

Some people hope that something like a Rosetta Stone will appear for the Harappan Colligation as well. But there's been no such luck so far.

But there's still time. Who knows, maybe you can be the one who'll help uncover the hidden secrets of the Harappan civilization by finally cracking the code!

WHATEVER HAPPENED TO MOHENJO-DARO?

SKELETONS IN THE SOIL (OR HOW AN ARCHAEOLOGIST GOT IT WRONG!)

As part of his excavations in Mohenjo-daro, the renowned archaeologist Mortimer Wheeler came across a layer that revealed several skeletal remains. Wheeler jumped to the conclusion that this was proof of a 'massacre' and that these people had been killed in an invasion. Wheeler assumed that this was how the Harappan culture declined: An invasion from outside. To prove this, he even cited some words in the Rig Veda to indicate that the Vedas were composed by those very people who invaded and destroyed the forts and other settlements of the Harappans.

Wheeler thought that certain references in the Rig Veda that talked of attacks on walled cities as well as the name used for the god Indra, '*purandara*' (fort destroyer), indicated that an Aryan invasion had, in fact, destroyed the Harappan culture. He even identified a place called Hariyupiya in the Rig Veda as Harappa.

For a decade and more, that was what was believed and wrongly too. Signs of decline do appear clearly in Mohenjo-daro by 2,200 BCE and it was believed that the settlement came to an end by 2,000 BCE. Also, since Mohenjo-daro and Harappa were the first sites discovered, evidence found here about their decline suggested that the entire Harappan culture had been destroyed the same way.

But then, as more excavations happened, and more sites came up, and a correct reading of written texts such as the Rig Veda was offered, Wheeler's suggestions were proved to be false. But no one really could come up with a good enough theory about how the Harappan civilization had really declined. Like its language, the reason behind the end of the civilization is also very mysterious.

The historian who gave Indian history a wrong beginning: Wheeler!

But can't we guess what happened?

We can try. And so many scholars and historians have! Around the same time as Wheeler's theory, there was another theory which said that the civilization was destroyed by Aryan invaders. This was because it was wrongly theorized that the people mentioned in the Rig Veda were Aryans, but the word came from 'arya' which in Sanskrit means 'kinsman' or someone who belongs to the same kin group. Some other scholars believe it was also derived from the word, 'ar' meaning to cultivate. The theory of invasion was first put forward by Ramprasad Chanda, an archaeologist and historian, in 1926. But he soon changed his opinion when he realized that other factors such as floods, decline in trade and over-utilization of natural resources could have had a role to play in the decline of Harappa and Mohenjo-daro. Yet he still insisted that the ultimate blow was given by an Aryan invasion.

Another factor was that the decline didn't happen at the same time in all the cities. The pace of decline varied. In some places, the civilization continued till 1,800 BCE. Dholavira, in northwest India, declined gradually, while at Kalibangan or Banawali (also in India), city life ended all of a sudden (we don't really know why). But precisely because the decline was not satisfactorily explained for several years, it gave rise to a lot of popular, incorrect explanations.

So what are some other theories?

For this, we must first examine why Wheeler's theory was debunked in the first place. This was not only because of the archaeological evidence that was unearthed later, but also because it was later found that Wheeler's interpretation of sources like the Rig Veda was wrong. Scholars such as P.V. Kane in 1955, George Dales in 1964 and B.B. Lal in 1997 rejected Wheeler's theory. One of the main reasons was that the Rig Veda is said to have been composed around 1,500 BCE, which is long after the urban phase of the Harappan culture had passed.

Plus, there are really no traces of an invasion, or of any kind of conflict at any Harappan site. But what about the skeletal remains that Wheeler found, you ask? Well, the 37 groups of skeletal remains found at Cemetery H of Mohenjo-daro do not belong to the same cultural period, that is, these probably appeared at different times, and did not happen all at once, as Wheeler had supposed.

Also not one of these skeletons was found on the citadel of Mohenjo-daro which was located at a level higher than the rest of the city (in order to safeguard it from intruders) and where a major battle would have taken place.

Moreover, if there were indeed invaders who came in foreign lands, their 'physiognomy' or physical structure may have been different: and there is no evidence to suggest that the skeletons found were in any way different from those found on other sites.

So Could It Have Been a Natural Disaster?

Well, we're not sure. Natural disasters did have a role to play but again, evidence of environmental causes has only been found at certain sites, not all.

In Mohenjo-daro, the presence of layers of silt (fine clay or sand found mainly along river banks) indicate that the city experienced quite a lot of floods (a lot like Mumbai in modern times!). The river Indus ran close by. Some archaeologists and scientists have argued that these floods happened because of earth movements, such as earthquakes. George Dales suggested that these movements occurred at a place called Sehwan, which is 120 kilometres south of Mohenjo-daro, where evidence clearly shows a shift of rock plates on the earth's crust. Perhaps this created a giant natural dam that blocked the flow of the Indus to the sea, turning the area around Mohenjo-daro into a huge lake.

But this theory isn't very convincing because it would mean that the Indus would have to be flooded repeatedly in order to destroy an entire city. Another theory, which suggests that the

Indus shifted its course and moved some distance east, which led to a water shortage, is also a little unconvincing because of the lack of enough evidence.

Sites around Harappa (which is to the northeast of Mohenjo-daro), in the Ghaggar-Hakra valley (in west Pakistan) were indeed affected by a gradual drying up. Earth movements here led to river 'capture': either the river Yamuna moved away to the east and then joined up with the Ganga system or (what is more likely) the river Sutlej began to flow into the Indus, and all this drastically reduced the water flow into the Ghaggar. A sudden rise in the Arabian sea coast in west Pakistan could also have caused floods and a rise in soil salinity (the amount of salt in soil), which in turn affected the coastal communications and trade of the Harappans.

EVEN MORE THEORIES

WELL, OTHER THINGS COULD HAVE HAPPENED TOO. PERHAPS THE HARAPPAN PEOPLE WERE OVER-USING THE LAND THROUGH OVER-CULTIVATION, OR THERE WAS OVERGRAZING AND EXCESSIVE CUTTING OF TREES FOR FUEL AND FARMING. (A LOT LIKE WHAT'S HAPPENING NOW... WE DON'T REALLY LEARN FROM HISTORY NOW, DO WE?)

MAYBE THERE WAS OVER POPULATION (IT SEEMS THIS PROBLEM IS AS OLD AS INDIA!) AND THE NUMBER OF PEOPLE AND CATTLE COULD NOT BE SUPPORTED WITH THE AVAILABLE RESOURCES (FOOD, WATER, SPACE TO LIVE ETC.). MAYBE IT WAS BECAUSE OF ECONOMIC REASONS: ONE SCHOLAR HAS ARGUED THAT THE DECLINE IN THE TRADE OF LAPIS LAZULI (A DEEP BLUE SEMI-PRECIOUS STONE) WITH MESOPOTAMIA WAS A FACTOR IN THE DECLINE.

SO WAS IT A SUDDEN DEATH OR A SLOW, PAINFUL ONE?

Archaeological evidence suggests that the Harappan culture underwent a gradual decline. It was in no way sudden. There were new people coming in, (as evidenced by new kinds of pottery that were found) but they certainly did not come as invaders.

These new migrants probably belonged to Indo-Aryans who came from Iran into India through the mountains in the north west, or some other tribe that were pushed out by the Indo-Aryans. BUT there is no archaeological evidence which shows that there was any kind of massive battle between the Indo-Aryans and the Harappans.

The period between 2,000-2,500 BCE still remains a mystery. This 1,500-year gap appears during the time the Harappan cities declined and when a different set of archaeological evidence emerged from other sites in the north that were not so urban as the Harappan culture. So, for a long time, we assumed that the Harappan culture declined with the coming of the Indo-Aryans. But no one really knows what happened in the middle.

But who were these mysterious Indo-Aryans anyway? Find out in the next chapter!

WHO ON EARTH WERE THE INDO-ARYANS?

THE PROBLEM POSED BY THE VEDAS

Before archaeology emerged only a few decades ago, India's history was all about textual sources, and the Vedas were the earliest of these. But the Vedas are religious and ritualistic texts and are not very historically accurate. They are also orally composed, which means that they were passed down by word of mouth (yes, they used to memorize entire *books*, and we have trouble remembering phone numbers!) and were written down only centuries later. Many historians say that the earliest sections of the Rig Veda, the earliest Veda, can be dated to roughly between 1,200-1,000 BCE or 1,500-1,000 BCE.

That's not to say that the Vedas are completely inaccurate. They do shed some light on the kind of life the Indus Valley people lived, but they need to be confirmed by archaeological findings.

For many years, thanks to Wheeler's mistake (and if you came in late, find out what that was in the previous chapter), we thought that the people mentioned in the Vedas were Aryans. But from the late 1980s onward, there was a more systematic study of these texts, balancing these with evidence provided by archaeology. It is now clear that it were the *Indo*-Aryans, that is, people speaking a certain kind of language, part of the Indo-Aryan group of languages, who were described in the Vedas.

Languages too come in families. They are grouped thus based on phonetics (how words sound), the meanings attached to words and various other criteria. So the people speaking the Indo-Aryan languages had some similarities in their language, as we shall see. So it's incorrect to call the people mentioned in the Vedas as the Aryans. So thanks to scholars of historical linguistics (study of languages), we do know that it was the Indo-Aryans who moved over centuries in waves to the subcontinent. To call them Aryans is misleading.

BUT WEREN'T THE ARYANS, LIKE, A RACE OF PEOPLE?

Well, no. But this is a common myth. Let's see where this originated:

It all began when the Aryans were identified as the people in the Vedas. Not only that, the Aryans were also wrongly defined as a *race*. This silly mistake happened, according to one version, because the word 'Aryan' is derived from the word 'arya', a word used frequently by the composers of the Rig Veda.

In the nineteenth and early twentieth century, as we found out more and more about our planet's history, historians went crazy trying to fit everything into neat little boxes. They were particularly interested in labelling people: grouping a bunch of people with common features (physical and cultural) under a general umbrella term. So a number of racial groups emerged: like the Caucasian, Mongoloid, Negroid, Australoid etc.

PHRENOLOGY

IT WAS A PSEUDOSCIENCE (THAT IS, NOT REALLY SCIENCE, BUT *PRETENDING* TO BE) THAT BECAME POPULAR IN THE NINETIETH CENTURY. IT WAS A SUBJECT WHERE THE HUMAN SKULL WAS STUDIED CAREFULLY TO FIND OUT WHAT KIND OF A PERSON YOU WERE. (WHICH IS, OF COURSE, COMPLETE NONSENSE WHEN WE THINK ABOUT IT NOW: RACE HAS NOTHING TO DO WITH WHAT KIND OF A PERSON WE ARE!)

SO, BASICALLY, ALL THIS 'SCIENCE' STUFF WAS PRETTY RACIST. IT WAS

ALSO A WAY IN WHICH OUR COLONIZERS (YOU KNOW, LIKE THE BRITISH) JUSTIFIED COLONIZING OTHER COUNTRIES: THEY THOUGHT THEY WERE THE SUPERIOR RACE, AND THAT THEY HAD A *RIGHT* TO DOMINATE INFERIOR RACES (WHICH WAS ALL UTTERLY RIDICULOUS, AND ONLY A PREJUDICE THEY HAD AGAINST NON-WHITE PEOPLE).

Anyway, coming back to the original question, both in India and Europe, Aryans were thought of as a race. It was believed that they all had similar traits and since they had been described as 'noble', people thought that they had done great things, and were, overall, a very superior race (almost like superheroes, but without any, well, superpowers). This myth soon became more and more popular, and before we knew it, Adolf Hitler of Nazi Germany was glorifying the Aryans over all other races...and we all know where that went (and if you don't, look him up. You'll be horrified!).

In the nineteenth century, when India was under the British rule, there were many people who glorified the Aryan culture, and believed it was the root of all great Indian traditions. Many authors and political activists also thought that India was the homeland of the Aryans although there was hardly any evidence to support this.

BUT WHERE DID THE ARYANS COME FROM?

Over the years many original homelands of the Aryans were suggested one after the other. These included Tibet, Afghanistan, the Aral Sea, Iran, Caspian Sea, the Black Sea, the Arctic, Lithuania, the Caucasus, the Urals, the Volga mountains, southern Russia, central Asian steppes, West Asia, Turkey, Scandinavia, Finland, Sweden, the Baltic region, and India. Balgangadhar Tilak, the political leader, even wrote that they originally lived in the Arctic! But none of these claims were supported by convincing evidence.

They came, they saw, but did they really conquer?

SO IF THE ARYANS AREN'T A RACE, WHAT ARE THEY?

So, basically, what historians now believe, is that instead of labelling a group of people based on their physical attributes, it's much easier (and definitely more historically accurate) to group them according to the language they spoke. (And it avoids all the racism that we saw before, about the Aryans being all-powerful and stuff.)

Today, most historians have discarded the idea of an Aryan invasion of the Indian subcontinent in favour of a history of waves, several of them, of *Indo-Aryan* migrations and movements of people. The Indo-Aryans were people who belonged to the same linguistic family or spoke languages with similar traits to each other. The Indo-Aryans, especially, were the speakers of a sub-group of the Indo-Iranian branch of languages that, in turn, came from the Indo-European family of languages.

WHAT ABOUT THE 'ARYA'S MENTIONED IN THE VEDAS?

WELL, THE WORD 'ARYA' USED IN THE VEDAS ACTUALLY MEANS KINSMAN OR COMPANION (SOMEONE FROM THE SAME FAMILY) AND IT MAY BE AS A WORD, DERIVED FROM 'AR' (TO CULTIVATE). IT DOES NOT DENOTE THE ARYANS IN ANY WAY.

WHAT LANGUAGE DID THESE GUYS SPEAK?

The Indo-European languages is a broad family of languages that includes Sanskrit, Avestan (old Iranian), Latin, Greek, Germanic (German, English, Swedish), Slav (Russian, Polish) and Romance (Italian, Spanish, French, Rumanian). Sanskrit and Old Iranian are even more closely related to an earlier language called Indo-Iranian, part of the Indo-European group. Indo-Aryans were again a subgroup of the people who spoke Indo-Iranian. Think of it like a three-tiered figure, almost like a family tree, with Indo-European at the top, and this branches off into smaller families, one of these being Indo-Iranian, and the latter again leads off to form the Indo-Aryan group.

On the basis of the similarity between these languages, historians thought that it was likely that the original speakers of Indo-European had a common homeland, probably the plains of Eastern Europe, especially in the area north of the Black Sea. But while they could have a common place of origin, we don't really know when or why the Indo-Iranians and the sub-group Indo-Aryans parted ways.

There is also no agreement on the routes or the timing of when these people migrated into South Asia, and India. In India, the Indo-Aryan languages also include the non-Sanskritic or Dardic languages, spoken in the mountains of the northwest, and this could mean that there was an earlier wave of Indo-Aryan immigrants. Superior military technology and the use of the horse and the chariot may have given them an advantage, helping them establish their dominance in the land of seven rivers, that is, the Punjab. But by this time, the Harappan culture and its cities had declined and the settlements here were now largely agricultural. There must have been interactions between these two different groups but they were probably not violent. Over time, a mingling of their languages must have happened as well, which makes sense, because there are also 300 clearly non-Indo-European words in the Rig Veda. So the Rig Vedic people were interacting with people who spoke a different language and culture, which ultimately led to the languages we speak today.

Pretty cool, huh?

DID THE GREAT WAR IN THE MAHABHARATA REALLY HAPPEN?

THE STORY OF THE MAHABHARATA

If you know your history (or if you've seen a TV adaptation of the Mahabharata) you'll know that a great war between warring cousins (called the Kauravas and Pandavas) was fought in Kurukshetra ages ago. It forms the largest part of the story of the Mahabharata. But there remains a mystery about when the war happened. Did it really happen at all? Or is it just a mythological story?

Well, first let's examine *where* the battle happened, or could have happened. The site of the battle, as narrated in the Mahabharata, tells us that the Indo-Aryans had now spread into the Gangetic Doab (doab is a place where two river meet). This is a time that corresponds to the Later Vedic period, when the later Vedas were written. The Rig Veda, which is the oldest, when read alongside archaeological evidence, tells us that Indo-Aryans had moved somewhat west, that is, the Punjab and the Indus region. The Rig Veda also mentions a battle of ten kings: Sudas, king of the Bharata tribe, displeases the sage Vishwamitra, who then forms a union of ten tribes to fight Sudas and punish him for his arrogance.

Scholars believe that the Mahabharata, and the cities and villages it mentions, shows us that the tribes or groups had begun to move eastwards. The later Vedic sources that are contemporary with events described in the two epics, the Mahabharata and the Ramayana, seem to have a wider knowledge of Indian geography; they mention the two seas, the Himalayas and Vindhya mountains and generally the entire Indo-Gangetic plains.

But sites that have been excavated in these areas show very little evidence of a battle. *Does archaeology then prove that the battle never really took place?*

WHEN WAS THE MAHABHARATA WRITTEN ANYWAY?

The Mahabharata may have started out as a description of a local feud (an old word for a quarrel) but it caught the imagination of travelling poets, who moved from region to region as their occupation demanded.

The earliest known references to the Mahabharata and its central story of the war are found in a book called *Ashtadhyayi* written by Panini, an ancient Sanskrit grammarian. This dates back to the fourth century BCE. This may suggest that the core 24,000 verses, known as the Bharata, that describe the great war of the Mahabharata, had been composed by the 4th century BCE.

That's not all. There are many more 'clues' to the time of the origin of the Mahabharata. A Greek writer called Dio Chrysostom who lived around the first century CE also wrote an account where he says that Homer's poetry was known in India and sung by the bards. (Homer, for those of who don't know, was a Greek writer who is said to have written the two great Greek epics: the *Iliad* and the *Odyssey*.) This seems to imply that the *Iliad* had been translated into Sanskrit. Some scholars think that this is actually a clue about the existence of the Mahabharata at this time, and that Dio confused the Mahabharata with the stories narrated in Homer's *Iliad* which is also about a great war between the Greek kings and the Trojans (yes, people wrote, or sung, a lot about wars in those days: probably because there wasn't much else to do!).

Based on all this, the historian Upinder Singh suggests that the Mahabharata, or at least its core story of the great battle, was written between 400 BCE to 400 CE. The Ramayana, the other great Indian epic, is dated between the fifth or fourth centuries BCE and third centuries CE.

'Run for your lives!'
The epic battle in the Mahabharata: Was it true?

SO WHAT ABOUT THE OTHER STORIES IN THE MAHABHARATA?

The Mahabharata, it is popularly believed, was narrated by Vyasa. Most of it is told as a story or stories within a story and other stories unfold from the main one. But it's important to remember that the Mahabharata is not the work of a *single* person, and it has a number of episodes (some unrelated to the main story) which, historians think, have been added on over the years, but which are just as important as the main story of the war.

Some of these stories include the Bhagavad Gita, the story of Nala and Damayanti, even a shorter version of the Ramayana, and the story of the sage Rishyasringa, whose father was a sage and mother an apsara, who had a horn on his head and supernatural powers (you might even say he was an early mutant, like the X-men).

Soon all these other stories within the Mahabharata took on separate identities of their own. For example, the story of Shakuntala, the daughter of sage Vishwamitra, that is mentioned in the Mahabharata was rewritten into a much longer play by the Sanskrit poet Kalidasa, and was called *Abhijnanashakuntalam* (or, *The Recognition of Shakuntala*: much easier to pronounce). *Urubhanga* is another Sanskrit play written by Bhasa (who lived long before Kalidasa) and is based on the killing of Duryodhana by the Pandava Bhima on Krishna's secret advice.

BUT DID ALL THIS REALLY HAPPEN OR NOT?

We're coming to that. Some of the excavations relating to the later Vedic period may perhaps help us discover where the war mentioned in the Mahabharata really happened. Archaeological explorations and excavations at places mentioned in the Mahabharata, such as Hastinapura, Kurukshetra, Panipat, Tilpat, Baghpat, Mathura and Bairat, have shown up a kind of pottery called the Painted Grey Ware (PGW) which is dated to 1,000 BCE. These remains tell us that the people who lived here shared a pastoral-cum-agricultural lifestyle.

Hastinapura, the capital of the Kauravas, was recently excavated. A part of it was found to have been washed away in 800 BCE, when the river Ganga flooded over. This incident is referred to in the Puranas and took place during the rule of the seventh successor to the king who ruled at Hastinapura immediately after the war. Dating back from the floods, this suggests that the war took place around 900-850 BCE.

There is another kind of evidence from Hastinapura. Some other Puranas, called the Matsya and Vayu, mention a flood during the reign of king Nichakshu (fifth king after Parikshit, who was the grandson of Arjuna and became king after the war). So the capital was moved from Hastinapura to Kaushambi, farther to the east. Excavations at Hastinapura did actually reveal evidence of a flood in the Ganga after which the site was deserted for several centuries. But this may not be the same flood that is mentioned in the Puranas, because the dates do not tally.

The existence of Indraprastha, at least in lore, is confirmed because it is mentioned in texts that were written several centuries later. Another story about the Mahabharata says that Indraprastha, the capital of the Pandavas, once stood where the Purana Qila was built in New Delhi. Shams Siraj Afif's book, *Tarikh-i Firoz Shahi*, written in the fourteenth century, mentions Indraprastha as being the headquarters of a pargana (district). Around the same time, a fourteenth century stone inscription found in Naraina village in Delhi also mentions Indraprastha. Another book, *Ain-i-Akbari*, written by Abul Fazal, one of Akbar's nobles, in the sixteenth century states that Humayun's fort was built where Indraprastha was located long ago.

Excavations carried out at the Purana Qila between the 1950s and 1970s have revealed that there are several levels dating from the fourth century BCE to the nineteenth century CE under the soil. A few stray pieces of painted gray ware pottery show that a much older settlement was also located somewhere nearby. But it cannot be said with certainty that this settlement had any connection with the story of the Mahabharata.

HMM...SO WHAT DO WE MAKE OF ALL THIS?

Well, to be honest, archaeology cannot really prove whether epic events and characters actually existed in real life. That is because there is a VERY IMPORTANT difference between how history and literature is written. Literature allows us to build an entire world, people with characters, around an event. It has stories within stories. Archaeology on the other hand tells us about the general patterns of living, but doesn't really provide specific details. Moreover, there is much in the long ago past that has perished with time or been destroyed. We cannot use archaeology to either confirm or disprove what old texts may say about individuals and events. Because sometimes the truth is a lot more complicated than it seems.

All we really know is that perhaps a battle was fought in the Punjab between tribes that made up the Indo-Aryans and with time, over years and centuries, it took on more and more legends and became an epic (pun intended!) story.

HOW DID THE CITY OF DWARKA DISAPPEAR UNDER THE SEA?

A LOST CITY

Among the many cities the Mahabharata mentions, there's one called Dwarka. It was a city that was founded by Krishna. He moved there with his clan, the Yadavas, when they were forced to move away from Vrindavan when it was threatened by the king of Magadha, Jarasandha.

Dwarka was supposedly a very beautiful city. The Mahabharata says that Krishna built Dwarka at Kushasthali, which was a fortress located on an island in the sea. Then another fortress was built by the Yadavas at the mouth of the Gomati river in Dwarka.

The Mahabharata mentions that soon after Krishna's death, a bitter feud broke out among the Yadavas and it was Arjuna (of the Pandavas) who came to the rescue of the Yadava princesses. But it was of no use. The feud and what happened later was all because of a sage's curse on Krishna, and a sage's words especially in legends of yore have always had immense power. The city was submerged in the sea, as the story goes, right after Krishna's own death. The Vishnu Purana indeed mentions the submergence of the city in the sea. While there are legends associated with Krishna and his Dwarka, most of the temples in the town itself actually belong to the much later medieval period.

Archaeologists have always been curious people. They

wondered if there were some remains of the old (and supposedly mythological) city off the coast. Around three decades ago, excavations were undertaken by marine archaeologists in the area around the Gulf of Khambat and off the coast of Gujarat. Dwarka is right on the Arabian sea coast while Bet Dwarka is an island in the Gulf of Khambat, both of them in Gujarat's Jamnagar district. An Underwater Archaeology Wing (UAW), part of the National Institute of Oceanography, was set up in 1981 to explore the area.

MARINE ARCHAEOLOGY

MARINE ARCHAEOLOGY OR UNDERWATER ARCHAEOLOGY IS A MORE SPECIALIZED BRANCH OF ARCHAEOLOGY. IT'S INVALUABLE IN THE STUDY OF OLD HUMAN INTERACTIONS WITH THE SEA: LIKE DETECTING SHIPWRECKS, OR UNEARTHING PLACES THAT HAVE BEEN SUBMERGED (OR EVEN, IN THIS CASE, A LOST CITY!).

BUT FINDINGS THINGS AT UNDERWATER SITES IS DIFFICULT BECAUSE SMALL, LIGHT ITEMS ARE ALWAYS WASHED AWAY BY THE SEA. MOREOVER, EROSION REMAINS A CONSTANT THREAT. WHEN MORE DREDGING (THAT IS, CLEARING THE SEA BED BY SCOOPING OUT THE RUBBISH) HAPPENS THAN REQUIRED, A LOT OF EVIDENCE IS DESTROYED AS WELL. SO MARINE ARCHAEOLOGISTS HAVE TO BE REALLY SKILFUL AND NEED SPECIAL EQUIPMENT. AND IT'S NOT JUST ABOUT THE ARCHAEOLOGISTS: OCEANOGRAPHERS, GEOLOGISTS, GEOPHYSICISTS, DIVER PHOTOGRAPHERS, AND OTHER TECHNICAL EXPERTS ALSO PLAY IMPORTANT ROLES. THE BOATS HAVE TO HAVE UNDERWATER CAMERA EQUIPMENT AS WELL.

THE SCIENCE OF MARINE ARCHAEOLOGY IS STILL YOUNG, AND AS IT DEVELOPS MORE AND MORE, WE CAN FINALLY UNDERSTAND AND EXPLORE ALL THE MYSTERIES HIDDEN IN THE SEA.

WHAT DID THEY FIND UNDERWATER?

The excavations were led by S.R. Rao, one of India's leading archaeologists, who had earlier excavated several Harappan sites including Lothal in Gujarat. Dr Rao began the excavations at sea after he discovered the ruins of an old Vishnu temple as he worked with his team on the Dwarkadhish temple at the city of Dwarka, just by the sea. This was dated around the ninth century and had been found in the middle of a modern construction site. As Rao and his team dug deeper, they found two earlier temples, an entire wall and figures of Vishnu.

Marine archaeologists first surveyed a large area off the coast. This they believed had once been part of the coast but was later submerged in 3 to 12 metres of water. In the island of Bet Dwarka, not too far away, they found a wall that was *560 metres long* (incredible, isn't it?). The wall was believed to be from 1528 BCE.

They also found a seal (not the swimming kind; a *mudra* or marker). This tied up with a story in the Mahabharata in which Krishna had wanted every citizen to carry some sort of identity: a *mudra*. (But of course, without further proof, we can't establish anything for certain!)

The discovery of these underwater ruins, located at a depth of 40 metres and 9 kilometres away from the Gujarat coast, were announced only around 2001, after some certainty had been established. And these ruins came to be known as the Gulf of Khambhat Cultural Complex. The remains of the walls, since it is not continuous and broken down in places, actually do not amount to much and it's difficult to figure out what the layout or plan of the ancient city was. It is generally believed that the city was about a kilometre long and at least 0.5 kilometre in breadth.

SO WHAT'S UP WITH THE WALL?

Again, we're not really sure. The walls found were very damaged and there's been a lot of talk about its use. Some say that the wall was used as a kind of fortification (i.e. help protect from enemies) for this ancient port city, or to keep the tides away.

'Ooh, look what I found!
The lost city under the sea

The walls also had gateways and six circular or semi-circular bastions (a fancy word for the projecting parts of the wall) located at regular distances from each other. The bastions could have been watchtowers to emit warnings when necessary, especially when there were chances of storms at sea.

The other things found were stone anchors, iron stakes, nails and even pieces of pottery. Some of the anchors are triangular in shape, others rectangular, and most weigh around 100-150 kilograms. Perhaps ships were anchored against the walls, since many anchors have been found near the ruins of the wall.

Bet Dwarka was probably a satellite town, as we know them today, connected to the bigger port town of Dwarka. It's also possible that the two places were linked by a narrow strip of land that sank as the sea level rose.

SO WHY DID THE CITY SINK?

As usual, there is no clear theory as to why these two sites sank. It must have been because of the sea levels rising or land levels going down. It could also have been due to climate change or disturbances in the earth's crust. In fact, the Arabian Sea was 100 metres lower in those days than it is at present and it is said to have swallowed up entire forests!

SOME IMPORTANT FINDS

Archaeologists found the ruins of a house with lots of conch shell pieces. Other important finds included an old inscription on a jar and a seal made of conch shell. This seal carried an unusual motif: an animal with the heads of a bull, a unicorn and a goat. The design is similar to those found in the Persian Gulf area and perhaps indicate that the people of Dwarka had links to this region.

Apart from being involved in trade, it is believed that the people who lived here could have been involved in boat building, pearl diving (that is, recovering pearls from oysters under the sea...yes, way cooler than your average desk job!), and maybe metal working.

At both these places, marine archaeologists found objects belonging to later periods as well. These included remains of structures, stone statues, objects made of copper, bronze and brass, iron anchors and a wrecked boat. These finds were then dated by the thermoluminescence method.

THE THERMOLUMINESCENCE (THER-MO-LOO-MI-NE-SENSE) METHOD

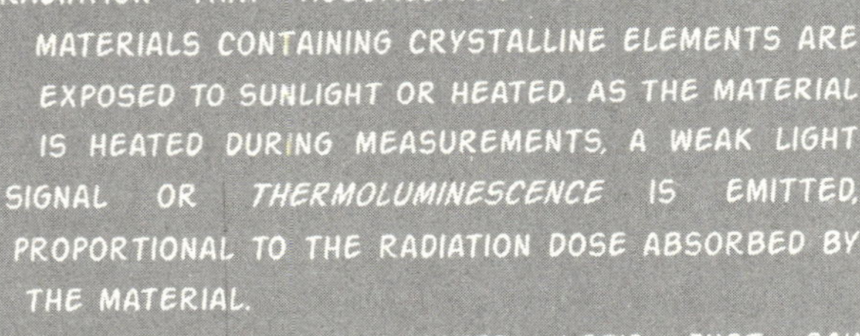

IT'S A METHOD OF DATING ANCIENT ARTEFACTS BY MEASURING THE RADIATION THAT ACCUMULATES OVER TIME WHEN MATERIALS CONTAINING CRYSTALLINE ELEMENTS ARE EXPOSED TO SUNLIGHT OR HEATED. AS THE MATERIAL IS HEATED DURING MEASUREMENTS, A WEAK LIGHT SIGNAL OR *THERMOLUMINESCENCE* IS EMITTED, PROPORTIONAL TO THE RADIATION DOSE ABSORBED BY THE MATERIAL.

(YES, IT'S COMPLICATED. LET'S JUST SAY IT'S A METHOD OF DATING THAT IS USED OFTEN BY ARCHAEOLOGISTS, AND YOU CAN LOOK UP MORE ABOUT IT ONLINE IF YOU'RE REALLY INTERESTED.)

WHO SAYS WHAT: THE USUAL ARGUMENTS

Well, there are believers and non-believers. There are historians like Michael Witzel who have argued that what has been unearthed are, in fact, natural rock formations, which perhaps drifted there owing to the tides. Others have said that a piece of wood dated around the seventh millennium BCE is not enough evidence of a lost city, because sea levels did rise and many other areas were submerged as well. This area is seismically active, that is, it's very prone to earthquakes and earth movement, and so the kinds of objects found, perhaps remnants of earlier settlements which were destroyed by earthquakes, are not unusual.

But of course, it's a *much* cooler story if the remains actually are from Krishna's lost city of Dwarka…and it's up to you what you choose to believe!

WHO EXACTLY WAS CHANAKYA AND WHY IS HE FAMOUS?

THE LEGEND OF CHANAKYA

The story goes that some two thousand and more years ago, when Magadha was a powerful kingdom under the Nandas, a man saw a young boy playing at being king with his friends. It was a remote village and far away from Magadha. As the man looked on, he was impressed with the boy, who sat on his throne high above his friends and made his judgements. He showed promise and qualities that impressed the man, who was called Chanakya, and who had observed all this while staying carefully hidden.

Chanakya would, in time, groom the young boy, who was called Chandragupta, to be first king of the Maurya dynasty, and help him overthrow the tyrannical Nanda rulers of the time.

OKAY, SO WHO WAS THIS STRANGE MAN?

Well, it's pretty mysterious actually. It is widely believed that Chanakya was the one and the same as Kautilya, who was the author of *Arthashastra* (which literally means economics), a famous old book on politics. But of course, as with most other historical 'facts', there were many disagreements about this. Some say *Arthashastra* wasn't actually written by one person, or even that it wasn't actually composed during the time of Chandragupta Maurya and Chanakya.

Anyway, what we do know is this: Chanakya was an ancient Indian scholar, teacher, philosopher and royal advisor, whose name is still synonymous with effective political strategy. He is well-known as a pioneer in economics and political science in India.

Most historians agree that Chanakya was a student and then a teacher at the ancient Takshashila University (now in Pakistan). He was also the mastermind behind the rise to power of the first Mauryan emperor, Chandragupta (remember that young boy from the story?) in 321 BCE. Chanakya served as the chief advisor to both Chandragupta and his son Bindusara. The Mauryan dynasty came about after the Nandas, the previous rulers, were overthrown, after an elaborate political strategy framed by Chanakya, as is believed. The Mauryan state was India's first empire, so to speak, and was organized on very efficient lines, with an army and bureaucracy that ensured that there were adequate checks and balances in place to prevent the misuse of power. The state as described in the *Arthashastra* is believed by several scholars to denote the Mauryan kingdom.

For his shrewd understanding of political and diplomatic strategies, Chanakya is often called the 'Indian Machiavelli', although he was much before Machiavelli's time. (Machiavelli, if you don't know, was an Italian historian and political diplomat, who is famous for writing a book called *The Prince*, a little like Chanakya's *Arthashastra*, and who is known for being, well, a little…unethical when it comes to grabbing political power.) Chanakya's works were lost near the end of the Gupta dynasty, that is, around the fifth century CE and were not rediscovered until 1915.

SO DID CHANAKYA WRITE THE ARTHASHASTRA OR NOT?

Well...scholars who have studied the *Arthashastra* in detail have attempted to shed light on this, but there are different views. The author of the *Arthashastra* refers to himself as 'Kautilya', while the last verse mentions the name 'Vishnugupta'. So many scholars believe that the former was the gotra or clan name of the author, while the latter was his personal name. Most scholars also believe that these names in turn refer to the scholar called Chanakya. While the various names attributed to the author of the *Arthashastra* have created confusion, it is generally believed that Kautilya and Chanakya are the same person, and that he probably lived between 370 to 280 BCE.

CHANAKYA: THE MAN AND THE MYTH (WHAT DO WE REALLY KNOW ABOUT THE GUY?)

There are several texts, including works of fiction that help to build up Chanakya's life, though some of it cannot be confirmed for sure. For instance, there are different stories about why he nursed a grudge against the Nandas, the dynasty that ruled Magadha for a century and a half before the Mauryas (that is, during the fifth and fourth centuries BCE). One story has it that his father was executed for speaking against the king, and Chanakya was forced to flee. Another story goes that he himself was humiliated by the Nandas because he helped himself to a seat of honour in the assembly, and he swore revenge.

There are many different accounts of his origin too. While one mentions that his father lived in Pataliputra, another says that he came from the south. There is one common factor, though, in all the stories: that he was widely known for his learning.

An early text that refers to Chanakya and his life include the 'Mahavamsa', a historical poem written in Pali (one of the languages used during the time) and regarded as an important Buddhist text. Jain texts from around the same period mention Chanakya's struggle against the Nandas: one of them is Hemchandra's *Parisistaparvan*.

There are also many works of fiction in ancient India, written much after Chanakya's time that mentioned him (yes, he was something of a celebrity!). One of the most famous ones is a play dated anywhere between the fourth and eleventh centuries CE, called the *Mudrarakshasa* (meaning 'Rakshasa's Signet'), written by the scholar and playwright Vishakadutta. It tells the story of how Chanakya helped Chandragupta conquer the throne despite all efforts of Rakshasa, a loyal minister of the Nandas.

THE MYSTERY BEHIND CHANAKYA'S MANY NAMES

THERE IS AGAIN A STORY ABOUT THIS. IN A BOOK OF FICTION WRITTEN IN 1939 BY PANCHAPAKESHA AYYAR CALLED *THREE MEN OF DESTINY*, BASED ON OLD STORIES AND LEGENDS SURROUNDING CHANAKYA, HIS WIFE GAUTAMI EXPLAINS HIS VARIOUS NAMES. GAUTAMI SAYS THAT VISHNUGUPTA WAS THE NAME GIVEN TO CHANAKYA BECAUSE HIS PATERNAL GRANDFATHER WAS ALSO CALLED THAT. KAUTILYA WAS THE CLAN NAME ASSOCIATED WITH THEIR PARTICULAR GROUP OF BRAHMINS. SOME WICKEDLY REFERRED TO HIM THIS WAY SO AS TO HINT AT THE COMPLEX (*KUTIL* MEANS COMPLEX IN SANSKRIT) PERSON HE WAS AND THE WAY HIS MIND WAS ALWAYS AT WORK, DRAWING UP NEW PLANS AND STRATEGIES. HE WAS CALLED CHANAKYA AS WELL, AFTER HIS FATHER WHO WAS CALLED CHANAK. AND THERE WERE SOME WHO REFERRED TO HIM AS DRAMILA OR TAMILA FOR THEY CAME FROM THE SOUTH, WHICH WAS KNOWN AS DRAVIDA COUNTRY. HE WAS ALSO CRUELLY CALLED ANGULA OR THE ONE-FINGER-HIGH DWARF BECAUSE HE WAS RATHER SHORT AND ALSO VERY UNREMARKABLE IN APPEARANCE.

IS THERE ONLY ONE VERSION OF THE *ARTHASHASTRA*?

The *Arthashastra* is actually a compilation of fifteen separate books called adikaranas. It is a long and complex work, with a wealth of information on revenue, budgeting, as well as on agriculture, patterns of trade and productive enterprises.

But wait, *Chanakya's not the only one to have written the* Arthashastra. His wasn't the only one that was written. Chanakya himself makes it clear in his book that there were other arthashastras before his, and that his work was only improving on all these previous lost works. But Chanakya's *Arthashastra* is without a doubt the most detailed. He makes systematic arguments, offering opinions of writers and schools before him (such as that of Manu, Parasara, Brihaspathi and Usanas) and also discusses his reasons for disagreeing with them. So, while Chanakya relied on other arthashastras, his was the most detailed and comprehensive one.

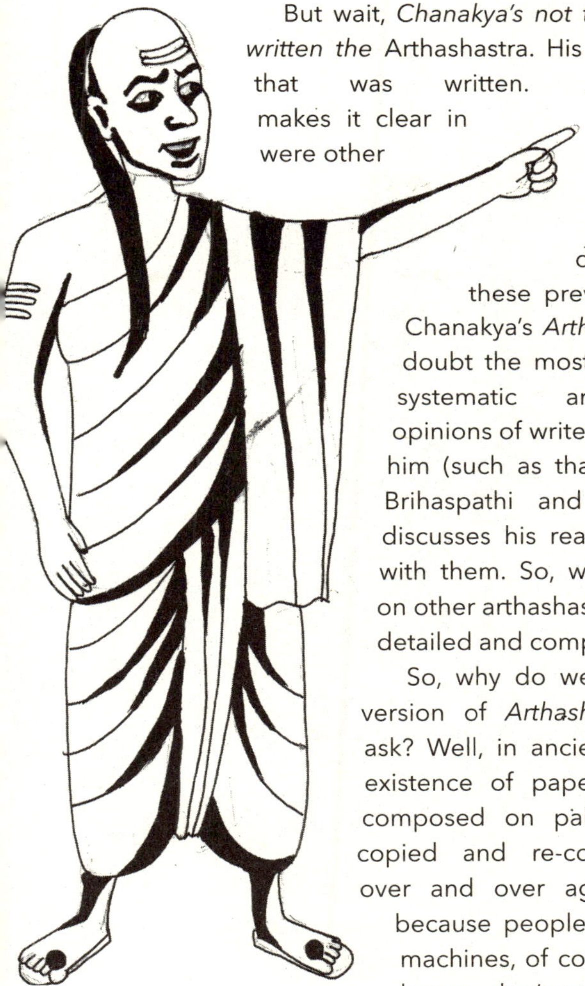

So, why do we only have this one version of *Arthashastra* available, you ask? Well, in ancient times, before the existence of paper, manuscripts were composed on palm leaves and then copied and re-copied several times over and over again. (Yes, by *hand*, because people didn't have copying machines, of course. We have it a lot better, don't we?) Scholars seemed to be doing this all the time. All the other arthashastras existed as palm leaf scripts before Chanakya (or Kautilya, as he's called in the book) wrote his more detailed, extensive one. Palm leaf scripts were not long-lasting and although Chanakya wrote on one too, because his

'You shall be king!': the king-maker and strategy artist, Chanakya

version was so exhaustive and detailed, people began to copy only his work, and the other ones were soon lost or forgotten.

In fact, the *Arthashastra* we know also narrowly escaped being forgotten. The story of how the book was found is also really interesting.

HOW THE *ARTHASHASTRA* WAS FOUND

IT WAS QUITE BY CHANCE.

FOR A LONG TIME, PEOPLE HAD COMPLETELY FORGOTTEN ABOUT THE *ARTHASHASTRA*. IN FACT, PEOPLE WERE TOTALLY UNAWARE OF IT ESPECIALLY IN THE CENTURIES AFTER THE GUPTA EMPIRE (FOURTH AND FIFTH CENTURIES BCE). IN RECENT TIMES IT WAS THOUGHT TO BE LOST TILL R. SHAMASHASTRY, A LIBRARIAN OF THE MYSORE GOVERNMENT ORIENTAL LIBRARY, DISCOVERED IT WHILE HE WAS TRYING TO CATALOGUE SOME VERY OLD PALM-LEAF MANUSCRIPTS! HE PUBLISHED A TRANSLATION IN 1906-08. THIS TEXT FORMED THE BASIS OF LATER AUTHORITATIVE WORKS ON THE *ARTHASHASTRA* BY OTHER HISTORIANS LIKE R.P. KANGLE, THOMAS TRAUTMANN AND L. RANGARAJAN. IT IS NOW CONSIDERED ONE OF THE OLDEST WRITTEN DOWN TEXTS OF ANCIENT INDIA.

WHEN WAS THE BOOK WRITTEN?

There are a lot of arguments about when the *Arthashastra* was written, and subsequently, we can't be sure of when Chanakya lived either, despite the dates that seem to be popular and which have been broadly accepted. Kautilya mentions early on in his book that it was written to end the misrule of the Nandas. Some historians believe it was written during the Mauryan period, but others think it was written sometime after the Mauryas. There are also other examples that point to a later date. For instance, the *Arthashastra* has no direct reference to the city of Pataliputra, the Mauryan empire or even to Chandragupta, so *maybe* it was written later.

There is also evidence that the trade in luxury goods that the book mentions, more specifically trade with China and Rome, happened much later. But most scholars have accepted that the *Arthashastra* was compiled more than 2,000 years ago, and while it may not describe exactly what the Mauryan state was like, its references to a big empire is almost similar to what the Mauryan empire under Chandragupta Maurya and his immediate successors grew to become. So, while there is disagreement over when exactly the *Arthashastra* was written, there is a general agreement that it can be placed at a time no later than 150 CE (the Mauryas, much weakened, remained in power around 185 BCE). Also a lot of historians believe that the book describes a hypothetical king, who would be ideal in every way, and does not refer to a specific dynasty.

To muddle up this mystery a bit more we could say that Kautilya and Chanakya may have been different people or the same. Perhaps the legends around Chanakya coalesced around the life of Kautilya, the scholar who wrote almost the definitive version of the *Arthashastra*, and the book remains invaluable, just as the stories remain enduring–which is perhaps what all good mysteries should leave us with.

WILL THE REAL VIKRAMADITYA PLEASE STAND UP?

THE KING AND THE VAMPIRE

If you haven't been living under a rock, you must have heard some stories of King Vikram and the Vetaal as a kid, especially from your grandmother. But are those stories actually true? Well, let's find out!

It all began with the King Vikram or Vikramaditya, ruler of Ujjayini, who insisted on being crowned king in spite of his ministers' warnings. They were worried because it had been predicted that an evil genie was definitely going to kill him on the very night of his coronation because this was what had happened with his predecessors (a pretty brutal way to die, right?). But Vikramaditya was unafraid and always up for a challenge, so he asked his ministers to crown him anyway.

There are some other versions to this story. In one, a sage requests the king to get him a vampire from the cemetery but every time the king picks up the vampire, it starts telling a story that ends in a riddle. The story is told, the vampire says, to ease the king's journey, but he always demands an answer in the end. These riddles are actually a test of kingship and Vikram answers them correctly every time. But nc sooner does he finish than the vampire slips back to the tree. The king trudges back to the tree twenty-four times but finds himself at a loss for an answer on the last occasion. This is when, as most versions go, the Vetaal reveals the sage's evil plot to the king and advises him how to catch the sage off-guard. The king manages to kill the evil sage and it all ends happily ever after.

Though there are many variations of this main story, in all of these, Vikramaditya managed to avoid the fate of his many predecessors, and in time proved to be a great ruler. But then here's the catch: as many as *fourteen* kings in ancient India took the name Vikramaditya. So no one really knows who the real king Vikramaditya could be.

WHO WAS VIKRAMADITYA ANYWAY?

The most famous of the Vikramadityas is the king Chandragupta II of the Gupta dynasty (yes, the ancient Indian dynasty that you've read in your History books). For all the significance of him as a ruler, his rule was considered a 'golden age', little is known about him. He came to the throne after the death of his father, the great Samudragupta and he ruled between 380-413 (or 415) CE.

There are several accounts of how he fought off the Saka ruler of Gujarat and the Kathiawar peninsula. The details of this actually appear in a work of fiction written several centuries after the event, called *Devichandraguptam* by Vishakadutta. In this book, Chandragupta is said to be the second son of Samudragupta, who comes to the throne after the death or murder of his brother Ramagupta. Ramagupta was first made a prisoner of the Sakas during his battle with them, and the condition placed on his release was that his queen surrender herself to the Saka king. Chandragupta disguised himself as the queen Dhruvadevi and once in the Saka king's tent, he killed the Saka king Rudrasimha. Ramagupta too died a while later. As the story goes, following the episode of the Sakas, there was a falling out between the brothers. Chandragupta pretended madness for a while and perhaps plotted to kill his brother, as the *Devichandraguptam* mentions. But then it is a work of fiction.

FINDING THE REAL VIKRAMADITYA

The traditions about the King Vikramaditya fall into two distinct categories. There are several stories about his bravery and magnificence: these are derived from the collection of stories called the *Brihatkatha* (literally translated into 'big story'), which were orally circulated (that is, there were no written sources, people remembered them and passed them on) in Prakrit, the language of the common people. These were later written down in Sanskrit. The *Brihatkatha* is believed to be the source of other popular books such as the *Hitopadesa*, *Vetala Pamchavimsati* and the *Simhāsana Dvātrimśikā* (don't be scared…it just means 'The 32 [Tales] of the Throne'). The last two books describe the King Vikram or Vikramaditya's supernatural and magical qualities of head and heart. The stories also praise his heroic achievements in a mythical way. They also mention his charity, and his association with the Nine Gems, noblemen who possessed dazzling abilities of various kinds.

These legends perhaps involved several different kings and over time, they were merged into the story of this one mythical king, Vikramaditya. The nine gems lived in different eras and periods so it is hard to believe they would thrive in the court of one particular king.

VIKRAM AND THE VETAAL, AND OTHER LEGENDS ABOUT VIKRAMADITYA

The stories of King Vikram and the Vetaal is a collection that has been translated into several regional languages and the best known English translation is the one by the scholar and explorer Sir Richard Francis Burton (he had also translated the *Arabian Nights* and explored Africa to find the Nile's source). The central theme of these stories is built around the tales the vampire tells King Vikram, and the riddle he asks the king at the end. In one of them, the Vetaal is impressed by Vikram's wise answers and he tells him how to foil an evil sage's plan to kill him.

'Answer me this riddle!' Vikram and the Vetaal could have been friends if only he stopped asking the king all those pesky questions!

THE LOST THRONE OF VIKRAMADITYA

BESIDES THE VIKRAM-VETAAL STORIES, *SIMHĀSANA DVĀTRIMSIKĀ* ALSO TELLS STORIES ABOUT VIKRAMADITYA'S THRONE, THAT WAS BURIED WITH HIS DEATH. IT WAS A MAGNIFICENT THRONE, EMBEDDED WITH RARE AND PRICELESS GEMS AND SUPPORTED BY 'THIRTY-TWO STATUETTES OF PRECIOUS MOONSTONE'. ONLY A KING AS PERFECT AS VIKRAMADITYA COULD ASCEND IT.

YEARS LATER, AS THE STORY GOES, ANOTHER LEGENDARY KING, BHOJA, CAME ACROSS VIKRAMADITYA'S THRONE AND WANTED TO MAKE IT HIS OWN. YET WHEN HE TRIED TO ASCEND IT AFTER A GRAND CEREMONY, ONE OF THE STATUETTES CAME TO LIFE AND PROCEEDED TO TELL HIM A STORY OF VIKRAMADITYA'S GREATNESS. SO SHE WAS BASICALLY QUESTIONING IF KING BHOJA WAS INDEED WORTHY ENOUGH TO SIT ON KING VIKRAMADITYA'S THRONE. IN TIME, ALL THE THIRTY TWO STATUETTES TOLD HIM STORIES ABOUT VIKRAMADITYA, ILLUSTRATING HIS MANY QUALITIES.

IN EACH CASE, BHOJA REALIZES HE IS INFERIOR TO KING VIKRAMADITYA, BUT FINALLY THE STATUETTES LET HIM ASCEND THE THRONE BECAUSE THEY ARE PLEASED WITH HIS HUMILITY. (MORAL OF THE STORY? IF YOU DON'T SUCCEED ONCE, TRY AND TRY AGAIN, EVEN IF WEIRD TALKING STATUES TELL YOU TO STOP!)

An entirely different set of stories are those found in the works of Jain literature. These talk about the king Vikram of Ujjayini who fought the Sakas in the first century CE and set up the Vikrama era, the calendar beginning from the year of his victory, to commemorate this event.

In these stories, Vikramaditya is described as the son of Gardabhilla, who regained his kingdom after he defeated the Sakas. The Sakas had ruled Ujjaiyini for four years. Vikramaditya commenced the Vikrama era after his victory and reigned for sixty years.

Another story, called the *Kalakacharya Katha*, written by (you guessed it) Kalakacharya, goes like this:

Kalakacharya had a sister called Sarasvati who became a nun. King Gardabhilla of Ujjayini, father of Vikramaditya, was fascinated by her and had her kidnapped (yes, kings could do things like that in those days. It's a good thing we don't have them around any more!). An angry Kalakacharya moved to the west, to the lands beyond the Indus and soon became very popular with the Saka chief ruling there because of his great astrological knowledge. Based on his predictions, the Saka chief invaded the kingdom of Gardabhilla and Kalakacharya himself joined the army that marched along Sindh and Gujarat, and laid siege to Ujjayini. The city fell and the Sakas established their supremacy over the region. After 17 years, Vikramaditya, son of Gardabhilla, regained his kingdom after defeating the Sakas. Kalakacharya rescued his sister soon after the defeat of Gardabhilla and after that, went to serve in the court of the Satavahana at Pratishthana.

This account has been related in other works too. In some it's mentioned that 135 years after Vikramaditya's death, the Sakas expelled Vikramaputra (his descendants) and conquered the kingdom again.

SO, BACK TO THE ORIGINAL QUESTION: WHO IS THE 'REAL' VIKRAMADITYA?

There is nothing else known about this king called Vikramaditya. He founded the era in his name and in commemoration of his victory over the Sakas. But his victory made him a king worth emulating (that is, following) and so other kings who came after took on his name.

It could be that the later Gupta king assumed this title and because he was associated with learning and culture, he is sometimes considered as the other Vikramaditya. But even Samudragupta assumed the title Vikramaditya as did later kings.

Another king who took the title of Vikramaditya VI was from the western Chalukya dynasty of west India. He ruled between

1076-1126 CE and came to the throne after killing off his older brother. Vikramadtiya VI is noted for being an appreciator of the arts. His court had many famous Kannada and Sanskrit poets. At his peak, the Vikramaditya VI controlled a vast empire stretching from the Kaveri river in the south to the Narmada river in central India.

There have been, in fact, no less than *fourteen* kings titled Vikramaditya till the twelfth century but who the 'real' one is, still remains a giant mystery.

Which just goes to show that names can be very misleading indeed. So if you're planning on doing something great when you grow up, choose an uncommon name, so that years later, historians don't get confused about who you are!

WHERE IN THE WORLD IS KAVERIPATTINAM?

THE STORY BEHIND THE ANCIENT CITY

The Sangam period is the period in the history of ancient southern India between the third century BCE and fourth century CE. It was named after the sangams, or assemblies, of Tamil scholars and poets of the time.

One of the most famous epic poems of the time is the *Silappatikaran* (or *The Tale of an Anklet*). It was written in the fifth century CE by the Jain poet prince Ilango Adigal and is set in Kaveripattinam (or Puhar as it's also called) at a time when three important kingdoms held sway in the south: the Pandyas, the Cheras and the Cholas.

The story of the *Silappatikaran* goes like this: Kovalan and Kannagi, a young couple, first live in Puhar where Kovalan, a young wealthy merchant, falls in love with a royal courtesan and neglects his wife who is devoted to him. But when they move to Madurai to start life afresh, he is suspected of stealing the queen's anklet. The story ends tragically with the death of all three but the husband and wife are reunited in heaven.

A second poem called *Manimekalai*, written by Seethalai Saathanar, is a continuation of the story. The heroine this time is the daughter of Kovalan and the courtesan. It tells the story of her conversion to Buddhism, under the influence of a Buddhist monk called Aravana Adigal.

Manimekalai, the heroine, flees Kaveripattinam, tired of the attentions of the Chola king Udhayakumar who is in love with her. She is helped by the sea goddess Manimekala who takes her to an island off the Jaffna peninsula, where a guardian angel gives her a magic begging bowl so she would never go hungry in life. The sea goddess takes her back to Kaveripattinam, where Manimekalai becomes the disciple of a Buddhist monk.

Where then was Kaveripattinam, the city mentioned in these two famous epic poems?

SO WHAT DO WE KNOW ABOUT THIS CITY?

From what we gather from various ancient Tamil texts, Kaveripattinam, also called Puhar, was situated at the mouth of the Kaveri. It was a very prosperous city. Early Tamil texts describe the Yavanas, or sea-faring foreigners, arriving with their cargoes in the city of Kaveripattinam. (The Yavana section of the city were probably very prosperous.)

An early Tamil poem of the Sangam period describes the town as being divided into two sections by a park and an open market which ran through the middle. The palace and brick-built houses of rich merchants were in the inland part of the town. The coastal half was inhabited by craftsmen, artisans and the less well-to-do and also contained warehouses and offices of the merchants. The foreign community occupied a separate area within the coastal section. (So very like the modern city, isn't it?)

These kingdoms of the south were by this time familiar with large scale trade by sea. The literature of the time has lots of references to harbours, docks, lighthouses, custom offices and all the usual buildings associated with ports. Though it does appear that Indians preferred to allow sailors of other nations to transport their goods, the Cholas retained a large share in the carrying trade of the Indian Ocean. They built a variety of ships, including light coastal vessels, large ships built of single logs tied together, and even bigger ones built for long distance voyages to Malaya and southeast Asia.

Kaveripattinam, in particular, was important to the Cholas. The Cholas, the Cheras and the Pandyas, the three early dynasties of the south, were at continual war with each other. The Cholas and the Pandyas came to dominate the east coast and were associated with the emergence of Tamil culture. The main area of their dominance was near the city of Madras (modern Chennai), and the state of Tamil Nadu gets its name from Tamil Nad, which means land of the Tamils.

OKAY, SO WHAT HAPPENED TO KAVERIPATTINAM? WHY DID IT DISAPPEAR?

Well, it's widely believed that the ancient town of Kaveripattinam disappeared in between the third and the sixth century CE.

One theory is that it was destroyed by a tsunami in the fifth century CE, that came about when there was a volcanic explosion in Krakatoa, on an island located near Java in Indonesia. This tsunami in the city is mentioned in the *Manimekalai*. The epic poem says that the sea god was angry because the Chola king had not performed the annual festival honouring the god Indra. This theory is supported by archaeological finds: submerged ruins were found near the coast of modern Poompuhar (in Tamil Nadu). Excavations here have also shown up coins with the tiger emblem of the Cholas and also a brick structure that could be a wharf (you know, that pier-type place at a harbour where ships are anchored).

The explosion of Mount Krakatoa probably brought about several changes in global climate across the world, according to new speculation by scientists of the Los Alamos Laboratory in the US. It almost brought about a mini apocalypse, what with agricultural failures, the emergence of plague and other natural disasters. It brought about the end of ancient super cities in old Persia, destroyed the Indonesian civilizations, the Nasca culture

The ancient tsunami that
(possibly) ate up a whole city!

of South America and southern Arabian civilizations. To confirm this theory, writings from China and Indonesia describe rare and strange atmospheric phenomena that possibly point to a volcano in the Indonesian region.

BATHYMETRY, THE STUDY OF THE UNDERWATER LAKES AND OCEAN FLOORS, HAS FOUND THAT A CALDERA (WHICH IS BASICALLY A CAULDRON-LIKE CRATER FORMED BY THE LAND COLLAPSING AFTER A VOLCANIC ERUPTION) SOME 40 TO 60 KILOMETRES IN DIAMETER THAT COULD HAVE LED TO THE FORMATION OF THE SUNDA STRAITS THAT TODAY SEPARATES JAVA FROM SUMATRA, AS SUGGESTED BY ANCIENT JAVANESE HISTORICAL WRITINGS. THE SIZE OF THE CALDERA INDICATES THAT THERE MUST HAVE BEEN A VOLCANIC ERUPTION IN THE REGION ON A TREMENDOUS SCALE. THIS, IN TURN, COULD HAVE TRIGGERED OFF THE TSUNAMI.

Was Kaveripattinam a casualty of this ancient tsunami? Despite all the evidence, there is still some doubt about whether the Krakatoa exploded in the mid sixth century CE. But if it didn't, what caused the ancient city of Kaveripattinam to disappear? Well, for now, we don't have the answers.

WHO DREW ON THE WALLS OF THE AJANTA CAVES?

HOW WERE THE AJANTA CAVES DISCOVERED?

In 1819, a British soldier called John Smith went hunting in the area around Aurangabad in the Deccan region of present day Maharashtra. He rode his horse across rough stony hills, stumbled through some thick vegetation and then came upon some very remarkable paintings on cave walls. This would turn out to be Cave X, one of the thirty caves that would later be uncovered in this complex. Of course, the local people knew about it. Even at the time when John Smith found it, they had turned it into a small temple, making simple offerings to the images that adorned the walls. It was also inhabited by birds and bats and, Smith suspected, by other wild creatures. He left his own initials on the wall (which is not something you should EVER do at historical sites, but unfortunately, John Smith didn't know better).

Over time, these caves were explored, and an entire complex of nearly thirty rock-cut Buddhist cave monuments were found, which dated around the second century BCE to about 650 CE. They were not too far away from Ellora: that also had cave temples but built at a later date. Unlike Ajanta, however, the cave temples at Ellora were never 'lost', mainly because they were very close to the trade route that was frequented by travellers and merchant groups.

The Ajanta caves are fascinating, not just because of the way it was discovered, but also because in all its caves, we can see the evolution of painting as a classical art form. What is more mysterious is the 'curse' that has affected the many attempts to replicate these paintings for an outside viewership. (Yes, a real, actual curse, apparently. We'll come to that later.)

HOW IT ALL BEGAN: THE HISTORY OF PAINTINGS IN ANCIENT INDIA

A story in the Mahabharata tells of Chitralekha, who was maid of honour to the princess Usha, daughter of the asura king Banasura. Chitralekha was a skilled portrait painter and was able to draw for the princess the handsome young man she saw in her dreams. It turned out to be Aniruddha, grandson of Krishna, who ruled in Dwarka.

In the Buddhist text called the *Vinaya Pitaka*, the dancer Amrapali invited painters from various countries and asked them to paint on her walls the figures of kings, traders and merchants seen by them; and the story goes, she fell in love with the portrait of King Bimbisara (well, they didn't have Facebook profile pictures to go by at that time, so portraits would have to do!).

The *Vinaya Pitaka* also mentions the palaces and mansions built by the king Prasenjit. These contained numerous 'chittagaras' or picture halls or galleries with paintings. Besides portraits and mural paintings, we also find mention of such widely known art forms as *lepya chitras, lekhya chitras, dhuli-chitras*, etc. *Lepya chitras* were stories drawn on textiles, while *lekhya chitras* were probably line drawings depicting patterns of a certain kind like the alpanas or rangolis that we now know. In *dhuli chitras*, the material used was powdered rice: white or coloured. Paintings were not only about religious themes but had scenes of everyday life too.

So paintings have been a part of ancient Indian life for the longest time. There are so many literary references to paintings in old texts that it must have been widely appreciated and practised.

WERE THERE CAVE PAINTINGS BEFORE AJANTA?

WELL, YES, BUT NOTHING AS REFINED OR BEAUTIFUL AS THE AJANTA ONES. BEFORE AJANTA, THE EARLIEST HISTORICAL EXAMPLE OF CAVE PAINTINGS ARE THE FEW ROWS OF HUMAN FIGURES IN YELLOW AND OCHRE EARTH COLOURS, ARRANGED TO MATCH THE SHAPE OF THE CEILING IN THE SITABENGA OR JOGIMARA CAVES IN THE RAMGARH HILLS IN PRESENT DAY CHATTISGARH. THESE FIGURES ARE DATED TO THE MIDDLE OF THE FIRST CENTURY BCE. ONLY A CENTURY AND A HALF AFTER THIS COMES THE NEXT PHASE OF INDIAN MURAL PAINTINGS: ON THE WALLS OF CAVES IX AND X OF AJANTA.

OTHER CAVE PAINTINGS HAVE BEEN FOUND IN THE CAVES AT BEDSA IN CENTRAL INDIA IN THE THIRD CENTURY CE, KANHERI (SIXTH CENTURY), AURANGABAD (SIXTH CENTURY), PITALKHORA (SIXTH CENTURY): ALL IN THE DECCAN. THERE ARE ALSO ROCK CUT TEMPLES MAINLY IN THE SOUTH AND IN SRI LANKA. BUT WHETHER SUCH PAINTINGS ARE FROM NORTH, SOUTH, THE DECCAN, THE STANDARD IS SET BY THOSE AT AJANTA.

WHAT DID THEY USE TO PAINT?

The paintings in these early caves have all been covered over by another layer of paintings that were added later but there are enough remains to indicate these murals were originally executed in 'tempera', that is a long-lasting even permanent, fast-drying medium used with the binding usually provided with egg-yolk.

Caves were first very simple structures, dug into hillsides and used as shrines by Buddhist monks. When a patron or follower made a generous donation, ambitious attempts were made to create in the caves something similar to the stupas built elsewhere. So the caves became more elaborate, with worshipping halls (chaitya) and monasteries (vihara), and then they began to be decorated with sculptures and paintings. In a matter of decades, the Buddhist cave temples at Ajanta and the Buddhist and Hindu temples at Ellora became the most impressive. Even the Jains joined in and excavated a few temples at Ellora.

Historians say that Brahmans and Buddhists vied with each other in cutting shrines and temples into the Deccan hills. At this time, worship at these shrines was open to anyone, the rivalry between the two religions weren't particularly felt by ordinary people. And while many of the paintings were religious, they also displayed various scenes of ordinary life. This technique of painting as seen at Ajanta is called *fresco-secco*.

HOW THE PAINTINGS AT AJANTA WERE ACTUALLY DONE

THE ACTUAL PAINTINGS WERE DONE ON A DRY SURFACE. A PASTE OF POWDERED ROCK, CLAY, AND COW DUNG MIXED WITH CHAFF FROM CEREALS AND MOLASSES WAS SMEARED ON THE WALL AS A BASE. THIS WAS SMOOTHENED OUT AND WHILE IT WAS STILL DAMP, IT WAS LAID OVER WITH A COAT OF FINE LIME WASH. COLOUR WAS APPLIED WHEN THE GROUND HAD DRIED AND THE FINAL WORK WAS POLISHED FINELY.

WHAT WERE THE COLOURS MADE OF, YOU ASK? THE COLOURS WERE DERIVED FROM MINERALS AND PLANTS AND STILL RETAIN SOME OF THEIR ORIGINAL BRILLIANCE. NATURAL EARTH, FOUND LOCALLY, FORMED MOST IF NOT ALL OF THE PIGMENTS. THE PARTICULAR COLOURS USED WERE RED OCHRE, VIVID RED, YELLOW OCHRE, INDIGO BLUE, LAPIS LAZULI BLUE, LAMP BLACK, CHALK WHITE, TERRA VORTE AND GREEN. ALL THE COLOURS WERE LOCALLY AVAILABLE EXCEPT LAPIS LAZULI (BLUE), WHICH WAS PROBABLY IMPORTED FROM RAJASTHAN OR OUTSIDE THE COUNTRY.

The murals in the cave temples may have been painted by monks although skilled artists must have been employed in most cases, since the ones in Ajanta look very professional and done by several skilled hands. The knowledge of this style of painting was, in turn, carried back by Chinese pilgrims, who popularized cave temples in China as well. Indian artists were also invited to China for their knowledge of cave painting methods.

WHAT DO THE PAINTINGS MEAN?

Ajanta's story can be dated back to a period before the first millennium CE. But only a very small fragment remains of this early phase. The early paintings are mostly of a crowded world of vegetation and flora, of gods and mythical beings, such as apsaras and yakshas and other grotesque beings, of the beauties of nature, of festivals and celebrations, etc.

Scenes from Buddhism also appear in many of the caves, especially those from the Jatakas (the stories that feature the many previous lives of Buddha, and have talking animals in them!). In Cave XVI, there are the three Buddhas, a sleeping woman and a dying princess, which is a story from the Shaddanta Jataka. In Cave XVII, there are the seven Buddhas, the wheel of causation, and Buddha's return to Kapilavastu.

One of the ceiling paintings in Ajanta shows an embassy of Khusrau, the king of Persia (590-623 CE) and his queen Shirin, that arrived at the court of the famous Chalukya king Pulakesin II.

Some of the more magnificent caves at Ajanta, with their brilliant fresco paintings, were excavated during the rule of the Vakatakas (an ancient Deccan dynasty), probably under their patronage, and the period 320-750 CE marks an important age. The Vakatakas ruled from their capital at Vatsagulma, which is now believed to be near modern Basim in Akola district (in present day Berar, Maharashtra). Some of the caves may also have been excavated by the vassals and officials of the Vakatakas. Caves XVI and XVII were the gifts of a minister and a feudatory of the Vakataka king Harishena. The Vakataka rulers were great lovers of learning and patrons of art and literature. After the Vakatakas, the Chalukyas continued their patronage.

The Ajanta tradition may have continued in other sites when work stopped, probably due to the defeat of Pulakesin II at the

What some of the Ajanta paintings look like

hands of Narasimha Varma Pallava in 642 CE and the chaos that followed in the Deccan.

CAN WE GET TO THE CURSE ALREADY?

After they were rediscovered in 1819, there have been many attempts to make copies of the paintings and display them. But all these attempts were mysteriously plagued by bad luck. In 1844-1863 the first attempt was made by Robert Gill, commissioned by the Royal Asiatic Society. He was a painter and photographer who made twenty-seven copies, but all except four of them perished in a fire in Crystal Palace in 1866. These four are now preserved in the Victoria and Albert Museum.

In 1872 John Griffiths and the Bombay School of Art made hundreds of copies of these paintings. His students used cheap varnish on the original paintings to make them easier to see, and this has led to a lot of damage. A lot of Griffiths's paintings were again destroyed by a fire in the London warehouse in 1885.

Between 1909 and 1911, artists led by Christina Herringham also worked on the paintings. She was the founder of the National Arts Collection Fund and also one of the founders of the Calcutta School of Art. But she later had to be institutionalized after she suffered an emotional and nervous breakdown.

But the curse is a relatively recent legend and perhaps mere superstition. And if you still haven't seen the Ajanta cave paintings in real life, ask your parents to plan a trip *now*, for you never know when these ancient paintings will disappear, like the caves that were 'lost' so long ago!

WHO'S AFRAID OF THE BIG BAD HUNAS?

HOW A DYNASTY FELL APART

It all happened during the time of Skandagupta, who was the grandson of the great Chandragupta II, or Vikramaditya. He came to the throne in 455 or 456 CE, he was the last of the great Gupta rulers. The Gupta dynasty had ruled for *three hundred years* over much of north and central India. But it declined because of Skandagupta's wars against the Hunas, a warrior tribe who came from the northwest. It's the Hunas who form the crux of this mystery. Nothing much is known about them or about their most famous king, Mihirakula.

WHERE DID THE HUNAS COME FROM?

To be honest, we know very little about the Hunas. They were probably part of a horde of Central Asian tribes, who were all warring and nomadic in nature. In the early years of the first millennium CE, different branches of the Hunas had already proved to be a terror to many kingdoms in both Europe and Asia. From the mid-fifth century CE, one branch in particular, called the White Huns or Hephthalites, came to occupy parts of Central Asia and threatened both Persia and India. They conquered the kingdom of Gandhara in Afghanistan and their king, Mihirakula, was known to be cruel. Soon they advanced still further into the heart of India and became a grave menace to the Gupta empire. Skandagupta had been successful in battling the Hunas during the long reign of his father Kumaragupta but these wars drained the empire's resources and led to its eventual downfall.

In records written at least five hundred years later, there are references to these battles the Guptas fought with the '*mlecchas*', which *might* have been a reference to the Hunas. Somadeva's *Kathasaritasagar* says that one Vikramaditya, son of Mahendraditya, king of Ujjayini, fought valiantly and defeated the *mlecchas*. The Buddhist text *Chandragarbha pariprichha* mentions that Mahendrasena, king of Kausambi, had a valiant son who defeated three foreign powers who had come from outside – the Yavanas, the Palhikas and the Sakunes. These powers had taken possession of Gandhara and the countries to the north of the Ganga. The prince of Kausambi was only twelve when he led his armies to a victory (yes, he was a brave, brave boy!) and on his return his father Mahendrasena crowned him king.

The origin of their name is also somewhat of a mystery. In Chinese sources, the name of the particular Huna dynasty in central Asia is referred as I-ta (from I-tien) and their king has the name Yen-tai-i-li-t'o (ancient Yeptalitha and hence the name Epthalites or Hepthalites). In sources from West Asia, they are called Eptalit. They have other names in Armenian, Greek and Persian sources. In Arabic sources, they are called 'haital'. According to one source, the etymology of the word 'Hephthalites' is derived from the language of the Bukhara, a tribe in central Asia, and it means 'strong'.

MIHIRAKULA: THE MOST DREADED OF KINGS

IN A BOOK CALLED THE *RAJATARANGINI* (OR *THE RIVER OF KINGS*) THAT WAS WRITTEN FIVE HUNDRED YEARS AFTER THE FALL OF THE GUPTA EMPIRE, THERE IS A REFERENCE TO MIHIRAKULA, WHO WAS THE MOST DREADED OF KINGS. HE RULED OVER BOTH KASHMIR AND GANDHARA AND CONQUERED AREAS AS FAR AS SOUTHERN INDIA AND CEYLON. HE IS DESCRIBED AS A VERY VIOLENT KING, AND THE TALES OF HIS CRUELTY

ARE TOLD AT GREAT LENGTH. SUNG-YUN, THE CHINESE AMBASSADOR TO THE HUNA KING OF GANDHARA IN 520 CE, WRITES: THE KING WAS CRUEL AND VINDICTIVE. HE WAS ENGAGED IN A WAR WITH THE KING OF KASHMIR. HE HAD 700 WAR ELEPHANTS AND IT SEEMED HE CONTINUALLY LIVED ON THE FRONTIER AND NEVER RETURNED TO HIS KINGDOM.

A LATER ACCOUNT IS BY COSMAS, A GREEK FROM ALEXANDRIA IN EGYPT WHO WROTE HIS BOOK IN THE MID SIXTH CENTURY CE, MENTIONS AN HEPHTHALATE (OR WHITE HUN) RULER CALLED GOLLAS WHO WENT TO A WAR TAKING WITH HIM NO FEWER THAN 2000 ELEPHANTS AND A GREAT FORCE OF CAVALRY. IT IS BELIEVED THAT THE KING GOLLAS IN COSMAS'S ACCOUNT REFERS TO MIHIRAKULA WHOSE NAME IS ALSO SPELLED AS MIHIRGUL.

BUT THERE IS NO CONSISTENCY IN THESE STORIES, NOT EVEN IN THE NAMES ACCORDED TO MIHIRAKULA AND SO THE HUNAS REMAIN SOMETHING OF A MYSTERY.

WHAT RELIGION WERE THE HUNAS?

Well, the Hunas, especially Mihirakula, are often remembered as a destroyer of Buddhist places of worship: they destroyed many Buddhist shrines and stupas. But we're not sure if the Hunas followed any organized religion. The Gwalior inscription describes Mihirakula as a worshipper of Pashupati, or Shiva, just as his father Toramana was believed to have converted to Jainism. A number of Shiva temples were also built in Kashmir during Mihirakula's time.

THE HUNA PLAN OF WORLD DOMINATION

The Hepthalites first appeared around the Caspian Sea or Central Asian region around mid fourth century CE. They spoke a language of the Indo-Iranian group. They were a war-hungry, semi-nomadic group. Soon they began to move south from Central Asia, towards Persia and India. Crossing the Hindukush mountains, the Hunas occupied Gandhara. They managed to set up an independent kingdom there in 460 CE.

They first encountered the republics located mainly in the foothills of the Himalayas or just south of these, in northwestern India (that is areas now in modern Punjab) and unleashed terror upon them! This was the time when Kumaragupta was the ruler of the Gupta empire, but he succeeded on the whole to keep his

*Kumaragupta:
The least known Gupta ruler was
also one of the bravest*

kingdom intact. Skandagupta, too, who came after Kumaragupta, inflicted a crushing defeat upon the Hunas.

But other places like Persia were not so lucky. In 484 CE the Hunas defeated and killed the Persian king. By the end of the fifth century CE, they had become rulers of a vast empire with their principal capital at Balkh (Afghanistan).

When the Hunas finally broke through into the frontiers of the Gupta empire, it had already become weak with the constant wars. The enormous costs of all these wars took its toll, and this is reflected in the coinage of Skandagupta.

After Skandagupta, the Gupta empire slowly eroded over the next fifty years or so. The kingdom gave way to several smaller kingdoms. During the rule of Budhagupta (last quarter of the fifth century), the Huna king Toramana launched an attack from Punjab, and conquered large parts of north India, reaching even up to Eran, in present day central MP. His coins show he ruled parts of UP, Rajputana, Punjab and Kashmir. Each successive wave of Huna invasion only made the Gupta empire weaker. Toramana was succeeded by his son, the feared Mihirakula, probably around 515 CE, which made things much, much worse for the Gupta empire.

WAS MIHIRAKULA EVER DEFEATED?

We're coming to that. An inscription dated in the fifteenth year of Mihirakula's reign (530 CE) shows that his kingdom stretched as far as Gwalior and his authority was acknowledged (read: feared!) further beyond as well.

But the Hunas were not fated to enjoy success for long and Mihirakula soon met his doom at the hands of two rulers: Yashodharman, who was king of Malwa and Narasimhagupta Baladitya, a Gupta dynasty king, also known as Narasimhagupta I, who probably came after Budhagupta.

Xuanzang (or Hsuan-tsang) was a Buddhist monk who came to India nearly a hundred years after Mihirakula. He wrote that Mihirakula was opposed by the ruler Narasimhagupta Baladitya because Mihirakula had been destroying Buddhist monasteries. Mihirakula in these accounts appears as a powerful tyrant who overran a large part of northern India.

Xuanzang describes Baladitya as a follower of Buddhism. When he heard of the cruel persecution and atrocities of Mihirakula, he strictly guarded the frontiers of his kingdom and refused to pay tribute. When Mihirakula invaded his dominions, Baladitya took shelter with his army on an island. Mihirakula left the main part of his army in the charge of his younger brother and landed with part of his troops on the island.

This was however an elaborately planned trick. Mihirakula was ambushed, by Baladitya's troops in a narrow pass and taken prisoner. Baladitya meant to kill Mihirakula but released him when his mother intervened. And Mihirakula, when he returned, found that at his absence, his brother had occupied the throne instead.

Mihirakula then sought asylum in Kashmir. But he stirred up a rebellion there, killed the king and placed himself on the throne of Kashmir. He next killed the king of Gandhara, exterminated the royal family, destroyed the Buddhist stupas and the sangharamas, plundered the wealth of the country and returned. But within a year he was dead.

Xuanzang visited India a century or so after Mihirakula and the facts of his stories are not all correct. But the defeat of Mihirakula finally crushed Huna political supremacy in India. For although the Huna community still existed, they were no longer a great power or even a disturbing element in Indian history: their power had diminished greatly after their defeats at the hands of Yasodharman and Baladitya.

As the power of the Hunas dwindled, the remaining groups merged with the locals: adapting their ways and customs. So finally, after years of rampage, the chapter of the big, bad Hunas finally came to a close.

WHO BURNT DOWN THE NALANDA UNIVERSITY?

THE STORY BEHIND NALANDA

The Nalanda University was the biggest of all the Buddhist monasteries in India, and one of the earliest universities in the world. It appears in ancient Buddhist and Jain books as a place where Buddha and Mahavira came and stayed often (a mango grove at Nalanda was said to be a favourite resting place of Buddha!).

For several centuries, it enjoyed great fame as a university that had students from across the world. But then it was apparently burnt down during an invasion by Bhaktiyar Khalji, a slave of Mohammed of Ghor, who later rose to become a military general in the time of Qutb-ud-din Aibak (who built the Qutub Minar in Delhi).

Despite this story, what is also mentioned is that in 1235, some forty or so years after Bhaktiyar Khalji's invasion, a Tibetan monk called Dharmasvamin visited Nalanda. While Nalanda had been damaged, looted, and largely deserted, it was still standing and functioning with seventy students. He also reported that a good many of the towers were still erect, standing as sentinels over a scene of desolation and ruin.

But its fame remained undiminished. In 1351, a monastery called Nalanda, in honour of the older university was set up in

Tibet. Tibetan legends continued to mention the great library buildings of Nalanda, especially about how it had been destroyed. One of these legends about Nalanda is dated to the eighteenth century, more than 600 years later. The story in this legend went like this:

Kukutasiddha, minister of the king of Magadh, had erected a temple at Nalanda. At its inaugural ceremony, two beggars turned up, and some naughty sramanas or student monks threw unholy water on them. This made the beggars very angry, who then performed a yagna (or fire sacrifice), and threw burning embers from sacrificial fires on the university grounds. Soon, everything caught fire, and before long, the three great temples containing the sacred scriptures were ablaze. But when everything was on fire, streams of water miraculously gushed forth from the Tibetan sacred works and put out the blaze in no time. The two heretics themselves ran from the fire but perished.

So does Dharmasvamin's story and the other legends mean that Bhaktiyar Khalji didn't really burn down Nalanda after all? Do these legends override the account of Bhaktiyar Khalji's invasion?

Well, the truth lies somewhere in between.

WHAT DO THE RUINS AT NALANDA TELL US?

Today, the ruins of the great university lie close to a village called Bargaon in Bihar. Excavations have revealed that there was a row of Buddhist temples on one side and a row of monasteries where the monks lived on the other, and there was an open space in between. The monks' cells had two rock beds and a niche in the wall for storing manuscripts (and you thought your hostel rooms were sparse, huh?).

There were a few other structures too. The remains of staircases show that some of these buildings had at least two storeys, maybe more. The monasteries were quite similar in design to each other. It seems that many of the temples and monasteries were repaired, rebuilt and enlarged over the years.

No more 'Back to School':
The ruins of one of the world's oldest university

EARLY TRAVELLERS' ACCOUNTS OF NALANDA

Nalanda is first mentioned in the sixth century CE. Faxian, the Chinese monk who visited India in the early fifth century CE, mentions the place but does not mention the monastery. The famous monastery/university was probably set up around the fifth century CE, after his visit. Monks who came later, Xuanzang and I-tsing, however, give detailed descriptions of the university.

Creating and running an institution like Nalanda wasn't cheap. Nalanda was supported by the income from at least a hundred villages and it was therefore able to provide free educational facilities and residence for most of its students (yes, free!).

The university covered a huge area and several portions were always being rebuilt, new constructions being built over old ones. Xuanzang's description mentions Nalanda's beautifully adorned towers, their dragon-like projections and coloured eaves, the outside courts, the carved and ornamented pearl-red pillars, and the rich decorated balustrades. The roofs had tiles that reflected the light in a thousand shades.

CAN WE GET BACK TO THE BURNING DOWN OF NALANDA?

Well, yes. As we've seen by now, Nalanda kept getting new constructions, and renovations were constantly being done. One reason for this, as studies have shown, is because Nalanda kept catching fire: not unlikely for a university that had so many sacred texts on brittle palm leaves (and at a time when fire safety was unheard of!). Dharmaganja, where the library buildings were, was particularly prone to fire. But most of the fires didn't cause intense damage. The palm leaf manuscripts and the wooden chests there provided huge combustible materials to feed a fire for hours.

Even when Xuanzang visited Nalanda, the original monastery built earlier was in ruins. At I-tsing's time only the foundations of this monastery were visible. Many monasteries in the long history of Nalanda must have been worn down by time or destroyed by fire or other natural disasters and treated in the same way as monasteries elsewhere: the old site not abandoned and new constructions built over the old.

On the ruins of bricks, one can even see traces of damage from outbreaks of fire but at the same time, they show that most of these fires (including the one talked about in Tibetan legends) were localised and did not spread across the entire campus. An inscription found in 1863 speaks of the restoration of a door jamb (which is a side post, by the way) after a fire.

But it's also evident from the ruins that all the architectural constructions at Nalanda were solid and substantial and although not fireproof, could not be wholly destroyed by fire.

SO NALANDA WASN'T INVADED BY BHAKTIYAR KHALJI?

It was! Well, the invasion theory about Nalanda's destruction also holds some truth.

The ruins of Nalanda have been widely attributed to Bhaktiyar Khalji, a slave of Mohammad of Ghor, who rose to become a general. Mohammad of Ghor's army and followers were all known as the Ghurids. As Bhaktiyar Khalji and the other Ghurids moved east, accounts say that they looted and demolished Odantapuri and Vikramashila monasteries. At the same time, it's clear they did not destroy every Buddhist institution in their realm. They targeted those that came in their path as they advanced towards east India, and it was a way of them showing off what they were capable of doing: of making an impact. Bhaktiyar Khalji especially had to make a point. More than wanting to appear as a great conqueror, his objective was to win acceptance from his fellow generals and commanders who had divided up the empire between themselves after Mohammad of Ghor's death.

The Nalanda University in Magadha, however, did NOT lie on the Ghurids' path of advance. For Bhaktiyar Khalji to destroy it completely would have required a separate expedition, and this destruction was (most likely) not their main objective. Even after the invasion, in 1235, as the Tibetan monk Dharmasvamin wrote, Nalanda still functioned with some students.

WHO EXACTLY WAS BHAKTIYAR KHALJI?

Khalji came from a Khalji Turkic tribe settled in South Afghanistan. He was more a mercenary (that is, someone who offers their services in exchange of money) and offered his services to various generals of Ghori. Some of these generals had once been Ghori's trusted slaves and called Mameluks. Qutb-ud-din Aibak was one of them and when he came to rule in Delhi, Aibak rejected Khaji's services. In Avadh however (in present day Uttar Pradesh), Malik Hasan ul Din offered him land and an estate in Mirzapur. But to support himself and his men, Khalji soon began carrying out raids into neighbouring areas. It was necessary because his troops needed to be paid and he needed his own army to hold his own against rival generals.

A SYSTEM OF LOOT AND PLUNDER

IN THE SYSTEM DEVISED BY THE RULERS OF ARABIA AND FOLLOWED BY MOST OTHER SULTANATES OF THE TIME, THE GHURIDS TOO PLACED THEIR TRUSTED MILITARY COMMANDERS AS GOVERNORS OF THE AREAS THEY CONQUERED AND GAVE THEM GREAT INDEPENDENCE. THESE GOVERNORS HAD THE FREEDOM TO COLLECT WHATEVER REVENUES THEY COULD COLLECT FROM THE AREAS UNDER THEIR CONTROL. THEREFORE, THE MILITARY COMMANDERS NEVER DESTROYED EVERYTHING IN THE PLACES THEY CONQUERED: SINCE THEY NEEDED THE REVENUE, IT WOULD HAVE BEEN STUPID TO HAVE DESTROYED EVERYTHING THAT WOULD EVENTUALLY COME UNDER THEIR CONTROL. AFTER ALL, THEY NEEDED THE MONEY TO PAY THEIR TROOPS.

SO THEY DID WHAT OTHER WARRIORS HAD DONE BEFORE THEM IN WEST ASIA: LOOTING AND INFLICTING HEAVY DAMAGE ON MAJOR RELIGIOUS EDIFICES AS THEY SOUGHT THE CONTROL OF THE TERRITORY. AND THEY WERE IN POWER, THEY GRANTED 'PROTECTED SUBJECT' STATUS TO THEIR NON-MUSLIM SUBJECTS AND COLLECTED A POLL TAX FROM THEM. IT WAS A GOOD WAY TO MAKE MONEY AND KEEP THEIR CONQUERED TERRITORIES IN CHECK.

Bhaktiyar Khalji, too, followed the same pattern. He rushed in with his armies, destroyed and looted, allowed his soldiers to amass as much as they could, and then he was on his way again.

From Nalanda he headed further east, to fight the rulers of Gauda (Bengal). More than conquest, he wanted to rule over his own territories, which was his way of getting back to all those who had rebuffed him and turned him away.

Yet his ambitions proved to be his undoing. He planned a conquest of Tibet and Turkistan further north. The Magh rulers of Assam pretended to collaborate with him. They let him through but played an elaborate game of treachery. Khalji's troops were ambushed and he escaped with barely a hundred men. Soon after, he was killed in his tent by a disgruntled noble called Ali Mardan Khan in 1205.

SO BOTH THE THEORIES ARE TRUE?

Yes, kind of. There is no doubt that Khalji's invasion caused considerable damage to Nalanda. But, as we have seen before, Nalanda was not new to fires, and they had kept rebuilding themselves after their fires. The Tibetan legend about the two beggars setting fire to Nalanda might well be true as well. But what we do know is that despite the invasions and the fire, Nalanda continued to function.

It did show a decline over the centuries and there were other factors at play too. This was a period of declining patronage, Nalanda had lost its earlier glory and they didn't have enough resources to keep running the university. The kingdoms of the east were also in decline. Monks and scholars had already begun moving up to China and Tibet or sailing to southeast Asia. Soon the thriving Buddhist scholarship moved elsewhere, and Nalanda was abandoned for good. Under a special initiative of several scholars and the governments of India, and the countries of Southeast Asia, the university of Nalanda is set to make a comeback, a modern university in every sense, to equal in time some of the world's best.

WHO KILLED RAZIA SULTAN, QUEEN OF THE SLAVE DYNASTY?

A KING'S DECISION

More than 900 years ago, a king in Delhi chose his daughter to succeed him. It set off a storm of protests. The Sultan Iltutmish had sons too and so what he had done was unthinkable at that time: women were hardly ever rulers in male-dominated ancient kingdoms. But the most capable of the Sultan's sons had died young and so he thought Razia, his daughter, was best suited to succeed him.

But Razia ruled for just three years. In a matter of months following her succession, a war broke out because her nobles opposed her. Razia fought bravely, even marrying one of her nobles in return for his support, but it was of no use.

She perished after a battle with her brother who had taken over the throne in her absence. It's not known how exactly the events of her death unfolded, and it also remains a mystery *where* this brave queen of Delhi now rests, because as many as three places have laid claim to being the burial site of the late Sultan, as Razia liked to call herself (instead of the female version of the word, sultana, which means 'wife of a sultan').

SO WHO WAS RAZIA EXACTLY?

After the death of Mohammad of Ghor, his trusted slaves divided up his empire among themselves and became rulers in their own right. They were called the Mameluks or Ghulams. One of them was Qutb-ud-din Aibak, a Turkic slave. Turkic does not mean they came from Turkey (despite the confusingly similar name!), but in fact means that they were part of an ethnic group that lived in regions of north, east, central and western Asia. People in the regions of Turkey, Azerbaijan, Kazhakistan, with similar cultural traits and historical roots formed the Turkic ethnic group.

The Mameluks rose to power in Egypt, west Asia and in the northwestern part of the Indian subcontinent. Qutb-ud-din-Aibak led campaigns into India and became the sultan of Delhi. This was the beginning of what was called the Slave dynasty. Iltutmish was Aibak's son-in-law, who began his career as a slave as well. But in time he, too, became a trusted lieutenant and after Aibak's death, Iltutmish made himself sultan in 1210.

Iltutmish ruled North India for twenty-five years. He faced the onslaught of the Mongols bravely during his lifetime. He also completed the construction of the famous Qutb Minar begun by Qutb-ud-din Aibak.

When his son, Nasir-ud-din, died in 1229 (he was governor of Bengal at the time), Iltutmish decided that his other sons were not very capable of ruling and so nominated his daughter to succeed him. She had, after all, been trained to rule and was as good, if not better, than any of his sons.

RAZIA SULTAN: QUEEN OF THE SLAVE DYNASTY

ILTUTMISH'S DAUGHTER RAZIA DRESSED LIKE A MAN AND INSISTED ON BEING ADDRESSED AS SULTAN. SHE COULD EFFORTLESSLY RIDE AN ELEPHANT OR EVEN A HORSE.

BUT THERE WAS JUST TOO MUCH OPPOSITION TO HER RULE RIGHT FROM THE BEGINNING, SIMPLY BECAUSE THE NOBLEMAN WERE OFFENDED

TO BE RULED OVER BY A WOMAN. (IMAGINE IF THIS HAPPENED TODAY, WHEN SO MANY OF OUR POLITICAL LEADERS ARE STRONG, POWERFUL WOMEN!) SO THEY STARTED CHALLENGING RAZIA'S RULE AS MUCH AS THEY COULD.

THE POWERFUL, ELITE COTERIE OF NOBLES CALLED THE 'CHIHALGANI' (OR 'THE FORTY') REFUSED TO ACCEPT ILTUTMISH'S DECISION TO MAKE A WOMAN HIS HEIR. AFTER ILTUTMISH DIED ON APRIL 29, 1236, THEY NOMINATED RAZIA'S BROTHER, RUKN-UD-DIN-FIRUZ, TO THE THRONE INSTEAD. RUKN-UD-DIN'S REIGN WAS SHORT. DURING THIS TIME, IT WAS HIS MOTHER AND ILTUTMISH'S WIDOW, SHAH TURKAAN, WHO CONTROLLED THE COURT FOR ALL PRACTICAL PURPOSES, WHILE RUKN-UD-DIN LED A LIFESTYLE OF PLEASURE. ON NOVEMBER 9, 1236, BOTH RUKN-UD-DIN AND HIS MOTHER SHAH TURKAAN WERE ASSASSINATED, AND IT IS BELIEVED THAT THE NOBLEMEN HAD A HAND IN THIS. THEY HAD BARELY BEEN IN POWER FOR SIX MONTHS.

IT WAS THEN THAT RAZIA CAME TO THE THRONE.

THE CONSPIRACY AGAINST RAZIA

As a ruler, Razia knew the rules of the game. She was able to effectively manipulate rebel factions against each other, and kept the nobles in check. But the noblemen resented her growing closeness with one of her advisers, Jamal-ud-din Yaqut. He was a Siddi, the people brought in from the east coast of Africa as slaves. Yaqut was an expert horseman and Razia appointed him as the superintendent of the stables. Next, Razia made Amir al-Umara (commander of commanders).

The nobility could not hold back their jealousy any more and soon a rebellion broke out. The provincial governors too refused to accept Razia's authority. In 1240, the governor of Lahore rebelled. But Razia was not to be taken down so easily! She gathered her forces and not only stopped the rebellion, but also chased the governor as far as Chenab and compelled him to surrender!

But soon enough, another rebellion broke out in Bhatinda in Punjab under Malik Altuniya. A battle between Razia and Altuniya followed, with the result that Yaqut was killed and Razia was taken prisoner. She was forced to marry Altuniya in an effort to regain her throne.

Meanwhile in Delhi, Razia's brother, Muizuddin Bahram Shah, was made king. What The Forty wanted was a puppet king: so that they could rule themselves, and Razia's brother was perfect for that purpose! It was also arranged that the government would provide the king with an officer, a Naib-i-Mamlikat (Deputy of the State) for at least one year. It would be held in rotation by different nobles from the elite group of nobles.

Altuniya and Razia attempted to take back the throne from Bahram but time was running out. They couldn't find much support for their cause either. They were defeated first in battle

'I'm as good as any man!': Razia the queen

on October 1240. Razia and her husband fled Delhi and reached Kaithal (in Haryana) the next day, where their remaining troops abandoned them. Razia decided to stop in Kaithal, hoping to regroup their army once again for one last attempt to regain her lost throne.

WHO KILLED RAZIA SULTAN?

Well, that is, of course, a bit of a mystery.

So Kaithal, where Razia had stopped, was an important historical centre. It was believed to be founded by Yudhisthira (of the Mahabharata) and also known as the city of Kapi or Hanuman.

Anyway, Razia then attempted to advance with a tribe of people in the region called the Khokars, the very same group that was believed to have murdered Mohammed of Ghor when he was on his way back to Ghazni after a battle campaign. The Khokars were an agricultural tribe and also served as mercenaries.

It is likely that Razia was killed by the Khokars or perhaps she fell into the hands of wandering thieves who roamed the area. Perhaps Razia and Altuniya were captured, robbed and killed. We will never know what actually happened, but Razia Sultan, queen of the slaves, was no longer heard of.

WHAT'S THE MYSTERY BEHIND HER GRAVE?

There are several theories about where Razia was buried.

Razia could have been buried at Kaithal or even Delhi. A third supposition is she was buried in Tonk in Rajasthan, where Altuniya and Yakut are supposedly buried as well.

What makes matters worse is that none of the graves attributed to her has a clear inscription or any kind of commemoration that can clearly identify her.

One of Razia's graves is believed to be in Old Delhi; in the city known as Shahjahanabad. It's believed to be near the Turkman gate, named after the Sufi saint Hazrat Shah Turkman Bayabani, whose tomb dates back to 1240 CE. The tomb itself is very neglected and hardly preserved. There has been unregulated construction around it. In the thirteenth century, the site of the tomb was a jungle, and no one knows how Razia's body ended up where it lies today. A second grave, believed to be that of her sister, Shazia, accompanies Razia's. Some of the Muslim residents of the neighbourhood have turned a part of the tomb into a mosque, where prayers are conducted five times each day.

The second claim is that Razia's tomb is situated near Kaithal city, Haryana state. The tomb lies in the north-western suburbs of the city where, a few years back, a jail was erected by the government. It is possible that her body was initially at Kaithal and later moved to Delhi but there is no record of this, in texts of the period or even later.

A more recent claim is that she and Jamal-ud-din Yakut were buried at Tonk in Rajasthan, where her father Iltutmish had once laid a siege. These claims were based on the calligraphy found on the tombstones, engraved in Arabic and not really clear.

But the mystery remains, since there's very little record of Razia's death: in fact, we're not even sure where and by whom she was killed.

WHAT HAPPENED AFTER RAZIA?

In case you were wondering, Muiz uddin Bahram, who had been placed on the throne after such conspiracy, did not rule long either (Karma, huh?).

His successor, Ala-ud-din Masud, had no interest in the kingdom, he lived a life of pleasure. It was after this that Iltutmish's grandson, Nasir-ud-din (who had the same name as his father, Iltutmish's son, in case you got confused) came to the throne. Nasir-ud-din Mahmud was known for his simplicity: he was a man of frugal tastes, and not much interest in being a king. So in all effect, it was his deputy Ghiyas uddin Balban who wielded power. It was only when Balban became the sultan after Nasir-ud-din's death that the powers of the Chihalgani (the elite, and evil, noblemen) were finally reduced, and the Slave dynasty rose again to its former glory.

WAS THE IMMORTAL LOVE STORY OF JAHANGIR AND ANARKALI REAL?

PRINCE JAHANGIR'S REBELLION

It was the year 1599, and Akbar, the third of the great Mughals was on the throne. Most of north India was under the Mughals and he was waging a campaign in the Deccan. This was when his oldest son, Prince Salim (who was later Emperor Jahangir), rebelled. It was because Akbar favoured his grandson, Khusrau as successor to the great throne. Furious at this, Jahangir rebelled.

Abul Fazal, Akbar's biographer and trusted nobleman, was known to always support Akbar's wishes, and in revenge, Jahangir had him assassinated by a trusted official. To ensure that the deed had indeed been done, Fazl's severed head was sent to Jahangir in Allahabad and the news later given to Akbar. Jahangir was finally forgiven and did succeed his father as Mughal emperor in 1605.

But there are stories that the real reason for Jahangir's rebellion was one completely different. It's a story that has become a legend. It's the story of Anarkali, the dancing girl who Jahangir fell in love with, and who Akbar never approved of.

WHO WAS ANARKALI? THE DANCER'S MYSTERIOUS ORIGINS

There is a tomb popularly known as Anarkali's tomb in Lahore where restoration work began some years ago. It's a pale white dome located inside the south-western boundary wall of the Punjab Civil Secretariat. The tomb is popularly said to be dated around 1605-06, built by Jahangir and as the story goes, it was supposedly built to commemorate Anarkali.

The character of Anarkali has always haunted writers and historians. There are some who say it is only a traditional legend that has travelled down the generations. Sources of Akbar's reign are silent on her. It is also surprising that Jahangir did not mention her in his book *Tuzk-i-Jahangiri*, nor did any contemporary historian leave any clue about her.

Most accounts of her, the first written some years after Akbar's reign, have certain common features. Anarkali was a slave girl in Lahore, and was a courtesan of the Mughal emperor Akbar and his son Prince Salim, later the Emperor Jahangir. She performed for Prince Salim at Akbar's request, and Salim soon fell in love with her. Akbar did not approve of the match and had her walled up within a fort in Lahore.

THE FIRST ACCOUNTS OF ANARKALI

ANARKALI FIRST APPEARS IN THE ACCOUNT OF A BRITISH TRAVELLER WHO APPEARED IN JAHANGIR'S COURT: WILLIAM FINCH. HE SPENT THREE YEARS IN JAHANGIR'S KINGDOM, BETWEEN 1608 AND 1611. ANARKALI HAD SUPPOSEDLY DIED A DECADE BEFORE THIS.

A LITTLE BACKGROUND ABOUT FINCH: FINCH TRAVELLED TO INDIA WITH THE GROUP LED BY THOMAS HAWKINS WHO WAS GRANTED TRADE PRIVILEGES BY JAHANGIR. AFTER MOVING AROUND FOR A BIT, FINCH REJOINED HAWKINS AGAIN AT AGRA ON 14 APRIL 1610. A YEAR LATER, HE WAS IN LAHORE TO SELL THE INDIGO HE HAD PURCHASED ON BEHALF OF THE EAST INDIA COMPANY. FINCH AND HAWKINS REMAINED AT JAHANGIR'S COURT FOR ABOUT A YEAR AND A HALF. IN 1612, THE EAST INDIA COMPANY SET UP THEIR FIRST LITTLE FACTORY AT SURAT AND HAWKINS RETURNED

TO ENGLAND. FINCH WANTED TO MAKE FURTHER EXPLORATIONS BUT HE DIED FROM DRINKING POISONED WATER IN AUGUST 1613, AT BABYLON, ON HIS WAY TO ALEPPO.

ACCORDING TO FINCH'S ACCOUNT, ANARKALI WAS ONE OF THE WIVES OF EMPEROR AKBAR AND THE MOTHER OF HIS SON DANIYAL. (IF ANARKALI WAS INDEED DANIYAL'S MOTHER, SHE WAS THIRTEEN YEARS OLDER THAN SALIM.) AKBAR DEVELOPED SUSPICIONS THAT ANARKALI WAS HAVING AN AFFAIR WITH PRINCE SALIM AND, BECAUSE OF THIS, HAD HER BURIED ALIVE IN THE WALLS OF A LAHORE FORT. JAHANGIR, WHEN HE BECAME KING LATER, ORDERED A MAGNIFICENT TOMB OF STONE TO BE BUILT IN THE MIDST OF A WALLED GARDEN AS A TOKEN OF HIS LOVE FOR ANARKALI. THE SURFACE OF THE TOMB, AS PER THE EMPEROR'S WISHES, WAS WROUGHT IN GOLD.

Based on this story, the present day writer Abraham Eraly too suggests that it was the mother of Prince Daniyal with whom Jahangir had an affair. He matches this with the story provided by Akbar's trusted court historian, Abul Fazl. Fazl writes that Salim was beaten up one evening by guards as he entered Akbar's royal harem (Akbar had several wives and mistresses, remember?) The story put out was that a mad man had wandered into Akbar's harem. Abul Fazl wrote that Salim had caught the man but was himself mistaken for the intruder. The emperor arrived upon the scene and was about to strike with his sword when he recognized Salim. What might be possible is that perhaps the intruder was none other than Salim himself and the story of the mad man was made up to cover up the prince's indecent behaviour.

But the problem with this theory is that the mother of Prince Daniyal had died in 1596 which does not match the dates inscribed on the tomb that was designed by Jahangir.

Edward Terry, who visited a few years after William Finch, wrote

Loving the prince didn't turn out too well for poor Anarkali

that Akbar had threatened to disinherit Salim for his affair with Anarkali, the emperor's most beloved wife. As punishment, he had Salim sent to Afghanistan and had Anarkali killed. An infuriated Salim rebelled against his father, and also had his beloved official biographer, Abul Fazl, killed. (Yes, a very bloodthirsty family, it was!) Finally, Akbar's mother Hamida convinced Salim to stem his revolt, for it could weaken the empire. Jahangir, after ascending the throne, had a splendid tomb constructed in memory of his beloved.

Other western visitors, who arrived in India during the next two centuries, only mention the charming gardens and fascinating architecture of the tomb, but nothing about who Anarkali really was.

OTHER STORIES ABOUT WHO ANARKALI REALLY WAS

Almost 350 years later, Noor Ahmed Chishti, in his book *Tehqiqaat-i-Chishtia* (1860) provided some details about the episode of Anarkali. He wrote that Anarkali was incredibly beautiful and hence Akbar's favourite mistress. Akbar's love for her made the other women of his harem jealous. Apparently Akbar was on a visit to Deccan when Anarkali fell ill and died and on the emperor's return, *he* ordered the creation of a grand tomb in her memory.

Syed Abdul Lateef, in his book *Tareekh-i-Lahore* (1892) wrote that Anarkali's actual name was Nadira Begum or Sharf-un-Nisa and she was one of Akbar's mistresses. She was from Iran and came to Lahore with a traders' caravan. As she was attractive, she soon became a part of Akbar's court and was given the name Anarkali because of her beauty. In this story, Salim is hardly mentioned.

In another book on the same theme, Kanhaya Lal writes that Nadira was a beautiful courtesan in the court of Akbar. Lal's story says that she died a natural death when Akbar was on a tour of Deccan. Later on, Akbar got a graceful tomb built in her memory, but it was destroyed and centuries later converted into a church by the British.

Abdullah Chagatai, an eighteenth-century historian and architect, wrote that the tomb that is supposedly Anarkali's tomb was actually the grave of Jahangir's wife Saheb Jamal, who was dear to him. As time passed, the lady's name was forgotten and the tomb came to be called Anarkali because of the pomegranate gardens in which it was built. (Anar, as you know, is the Hindi name for pomegranate.)

This garden is also mentioned by Dara Shikoh, Jahangir's grandson, in his work *Safinat-Ul-Auliya*, as one of the places visited by the Sufi saint Hazrat Mian Mir. Dara Shikoh noted the presence of a tomb in the garden but he did not name it.

SALIM AND ANARKALI AT THE MOVIES

POPULAR IMAGINATION HAS ALWAYS PICTURED ANARKALI AND JAHANGIR'S ROMANCE AS A GRAND, EPIC LOVE STORY, ON THE SCALE OF ROMEO AND JULIET, OR HEER-RANJHA. THE ROMANCE ASSOCIATED WITH THESE TWO WAS FIRST CREATED WHEN IMTIAZ ALI TAJ WROTE A PLAY ON ANARKALI'S AFFAIR WITH PRINCE SALIM AND HER FINAL DEATH. THE FAMOUS FILM *MUGHAL-E-AZAM* WHICH RELEASED IN THE 1960S ALSO MADE THESE TWO CHARACTERS IMMORTAL. ANARKALI WAS PLAYED BY MADHUBALA, A GIFTED ACTRESS THAT YOU MIGHT HAVE HEARD OF, AND SALIM WAS PLAYED BY DILIP KUMAR.

SO, IS THE LOVE STORY TRUE? WELL, WE CAN'T TELL. THAT'S ONE OF THE GREAT MYSTERIES OF THE MUGHAL PERIOD.

WHAT WE DO KNOW IS THAT PRINCE SALIM WAS SO UNHAPPY WITH HIS FATHER IN THIS YEAR 1599 THAT HE DEFIED HIS ORDERS AND REVOLTED.

SO WHAT HAPPENED TO ANARKALI'S TOMB?

Whatever the origins of the Anarkali's tomb, it was used by successive Sikh and British rulers of Lahore variously as a church, a cantonment building, a store house and even as someone's residence! In the first half of nineteenth century, it was the residence of Ranjit Singh's French general Jean Baptiste Ventura's wife, who was an Armenian.

From 1849 onwards, at the end of the Anglo-Sikh wars which

the British won, the area came to be used as an office for the staff of the first British Resident, Henry Lawrence. In 1851, the tomb became the St James Church. The tomb building also saw several modifications.

Forty years later, in 1891, the Punjab government decided to use the tomb as an office to house government records. In 1924, the government established a Historical Record Office here. It was later shifted but there is still a museum in its precincts.

But despite all the boring things that the tomb is now being used for, rumours and stories still keep the legend of Anarkali and Jahangir alive. Who knows, maybe the spirit of Anarkali, whoever she was, still wanders through the pomegranate gardens near what was once her tomb...

WHAT ARE THE PILLARS OF ASHOKA AND WHAT DO THEY MEAN?

HOW THESE STRANGE PILLARS WERE FOUND

It all began during the reign of Sultan Firoz Shah Tughlaq, who ruled over north India between 1351 to 1388. Once on his way to Meerut and Topra, not far away from his capital at Delhi, he noticed certain free-standing pillars. The sultan was so fascinated by them that he had them transported to Delhi, although it was very difficult in that day and age and even had one of them placed in a commanding position on the roof of his citadel. He was curious to know what the inscriptions on the pillars said, but no one could read it. He was told it was a magical charm and that it was associated with a religious ritual.

It was only five hundred years later that the script on the pillars were finally decoded. It was then found out that these pillars had belonged to King Ashoka of the Mauryas, who ruled 1500 years before the Firoz Shah. This was only possible because of the efforts of a band of scholars called the Orientalists.

WHO WERE THE ORIENTALISTS?

ORIENTALISM IS THE STUDY OF THE ORIENT (THAT IS, THE EASTERN WORLD); AND ORIENTALISTS WAS THE NAME GIVEN TO SCHOLARS AND ADMINISTRATORS WHO WANTED TO DISCOVER THIS 'OTHER' WORLD.

THE ORIENTALISTS, WHO WERE MOSTLY BRITISH OR NON-INDIAN, WORKED WITH THE HELP OF LOCAL SCHOLARS AND TOGETHER MADE AN EFFORT TO REDISCOVER INDIAN CULTURE AND HISTORY. TODAY, THE WORD 'ORIENTALISM' IS LOOKED DOWN UPON (BECAUSE IT DENOTES THAT THE WEST IS LOOKING AT THE EASTERN WORLD THROUGH THEIR PERSPECTIVE AND THEREFORE, NOT DOING A VERY GOOD JOB). BUT IN THOSE DAYS, THEY WERE REGARDED AS DEVOTED SCHOLARS WHO WERE INTERESTED IN EXPLORING THE UNKNOWN WORLDS OF THE EAST.

The task of decoding the inscriptions was by no means easy. Ashoka's edicts were found in several other places as well: inscribed on pillars, boulders and even in caves. What was even stranger was that everywhere they were written in the local script. In the northwest, around Peshawar, for example, they were in the Kharoshti script. In the extreme northwest of the empire, where they had been found near Kandahar, they were written in Greek and Aramaic. Elsewhere in India, they were written using the brahmi script, in the Magadhi language.

WHO EXACTLY WAS KING ASHOKA?

Ashoka was the grandson of Chandragupta Maurya, the founder of the Mauryan dynasty. The ONLY major war that Ashoka fought in his lifetime was with the state of Kalinga (which is now near present day Orissa) around 260 BC.

The Kalinga war was a huge and destructive war: over 150,000 people were deported, and more than 100,000 killed. In the aftermath of the battle, Ashoka became a very repentant figure. He was guilty of the violence and destruction he caused and his thoughts turned inwards, and he examined his life. He understood the need for peace and was drawn towards Buddhism and its message of non-violence. It took him two and a half years however to finally convert, and when he did, he gave up war as a means of conquest (and this at a time when kings almost inevitably waged several wars in their lifetime!).

The idea of making rock inscriptions may have come to Ashoka after hearing about those of King Darius of Persia. The Northwestern provinces had once been part of the Achaemenid Empire (an old Persian empire) and still retained many Persian features. In fact, the Ashokan pillars bear a remarkable similarity to those at Persepolis (the capital of the Achaemenid Empire) and may have been sculpted by craftsmen from the northwest province.

SO WHAT DO THE INSCRIPTIONS MEAN?

Well, the inscriptions of Ashoka are of two kinds. Ashoka made a distinction between his personal beliefs as a Buddhist and his duties as an emperor. A smaller group of his inscriptions consists of his declarations as a Buddhist. But a far larger group of inscriptions are edicts inscribed on specially erected pillars that were put up in places where crowds were likely to see them. These inscriptions put forward in detail what is known as Ashoka's dhamma or dharma, which means Universal Law or righteousness.

The curious case of Ashoka's pillars

What is the dhamma? Ashoka's dhamma was directed towards all his subjects, no matter what religion they followed, and tried to build an attitude that promoted social responsibility and the need for good behaviour of one person towards another. His dhamma emphasized non-violence but Ashoka was practical about it: he said he would not wage war and advised his successors not to do so either. But where conquest was essential and couldn't be avoided, he stressed that it had to be done with mercy.

Okay, so how were these inscriptions decoded?

It was an official of the East India Company called James Prinsep who played a lead role in interpreting these edicts. He was able to read the Brahmi script on the inscriptions, where he found a repeated reference to a king called Piyadasi. Prinsep, of course, had no idea who this Piyadasi was. But the answer came soon enough, when George Turnour, an officer of the Ceylon civil service, identified the king as Ashoka, on the basis of references in an ancient Buddhist book called the *Mahavamsa*, written in Pali language about the kings of Sri Lanka.

Then several years later in 1915, a British engineer called C. Beadon, prospecting for gold in Mysore state (present day Karnataka), found an inscription in a village called Maski (in Raichur district) which confirmed that the King Piyadasi was in fact Ashoka. On this inscription, both the names for the king were used. Another inscription found at the village of Gujarra in the Datia district of Madhya Pradesh, also shows the name Ashoka along with the usual 'Devanam Piyadassi'.

James Prinsep also played a role in the decipherment of the Kharoshti script, along with several other scholars. The decipherment of the Kharoshti script was easier because there were already old coins available which had inscriptions in both Greek and Kharoshti, and had been issued by the Indo-Greek kings of the early centuries of the first millennium CE.

JAMES PRINSEP: SCHOLAR, HISTORIAN, INVENTOR EXTRAORDINAIRE!

JAMES PRINSEP (1799-1840) WAS A MAN WHO HAD ALL KINDS OF INTERESTS, AND WHO CONTRIBUTED ENORMOUSLY TO SEVERAL DIFFERENT FIELDS OF STUDY. AS HIS CAREER IN INDIA SHOWS US, HE STUDIED, DOCUMENTED AND ILLUSTRATED MANY ASPECTS OF METALLURGY, METEOROLOGY AND HISTORY, APART FROM PURSUING HIS CAREER IN INDIA AS AN ASSAY MASTER (THAT IS, SOMEONE WHO TESTS THE QUANTITY AND QUALITY OF METAL IN COINS) AT THE MINT IN BENARES.

HIS FATHER, JOHN PRINSEP, HAD COME TO INDIA IN 1771 WITH ALMOST NO MONEY BUT HAD, OVER THE YEARS, BECOME A SUCCESSFUL INDIGO PLANTER. HE RETURNED TO ENGLAND IN 1787 WITH A HUGE FORTUNE AND ESTABLISHED HIMSELF AS A MERCHANT OF THE EAST INDIA COMPANY, BUYING GOODS FROM CHINA AND INDIA. HIS CONNECTIONS HELPED HIM FIND WORK FOR ALL HIS SONS AND SEVERAL MEMBERS OF HIS FAMILY ROSE TO HIGH POSITIONS IN INDIA.

FROM HIS CHILDHOOD, JAMES SHOWED A GIFT FOR DETAILED DRAWING AND MECHANICAL INVENTION, DESPITE HAVING POOR EYESIGHT. HE STUDIED ARCHITECTURE BUT BECAUSE OF HIS EYESIGHT, HE COULDN'T TAKE UP ARCHITECTURE AS A PROFESSION. HIS FATHER GOT HIM A JOB IN THE ASSAY DEPARTMENT AT A MINT IN INDIA.

PRINSEP REACHED CALCUTTA WITH HIS BROTHER HENRY IN SEPTEMBER 1819. A YEAR LATER, HE WAS SENT BY HIS SUPERIOR, THE SCHOLAR HORACE WILSON, TO WORK IN THE BENARES MINT. HE STAYED AT BENARES FOR THE NEXT ELEVEN YEARS UNTIL 1830 AND MOVED TO CALCUTTA IN 1832, WHERE HE BECAME ASSAY MASTER AFTER WILSON'S RESIGNATION.

AT BENARAS, PRINSEP CONDUCTED MANY SCIENTIFIC STUDIES (HE HAD ALSO STUDIED CHEMISTRY BACK HOME). HE WORKED ON WAYS TO MEASURE HIGH TEMPERATURES ACCURATELY IN FURNACES AND PUBLISHED HIS FINDINGS.

PRINSEP WAS ALSO A GREAT INVENTOR. HE INVENTED DEVICES TO MEASURE RAINFALL WITHIN A PRECISE .005 INCHES AND THE AMOUNT OF EVAPORATION WITHIN .001

INCHES. HE ALSO MADE DETAILED SKETCHES OF ANCIENT MONUMENTS, INSTRUMENTS, FOSSILS AND OTHER SUBJECTS. HIS EYESIGHT HAD SUFFICIENTLY RECOVERED, AND HE ALSO STUDIED AND ILLUSTRATED TEMPLE ARCHITECTURE. HE ALSO PAINTED A SERIES OF WATERCOLOURS OF MONUMENTS AND FESTIVITIES IN BENARES THAT WERE LATER PUBLISHED IN LONDON. HE HELPED DESIGN A TUNNEL WITH ARCHWAYS TO HELP DRAIN STAGNANT LAKES AND IMPROVE THE SANITATION OF THE DENSELY POPULATED AREAS OF BENARES.

ALTOGETHER, HE WAS AN INCREDIBLY BUSY (AND EXTREMELY TALENTED) MAN!

Coming back to our story, Prinsep came across the inscriptions once he became secretary of the Asiatic Society in Calcutta. Prinsep at once appealed to officers in the area to send him more coins and inscriptions. His appeal was enormously successful. In no time, he was flooded with coins and inscriptions: materials that would soon change the course of Indian history as we knew it then.

The coins were what first caught Prinsep's interest. He interpreted the Bactrian and Kusana coins from the northwest, and then all the local Indian ones. But the achievement for which he will always be best known is the decoding of the Brahmi script. Of course, much of the Brahmi script (especially the medieval Brahmi script) had already been decoded before Prinsep's final achievement. But his efforts uncovered this enduring mystery once and for all.

George Turnour also played a memorable role in identifying the king Ashoka. He was a British civil servant, scholar and a historian. He was known for his translation of the *Mahavamsa* that was published in 1837. Along with James Prinsep and others, he began to decipher the inscriptions on the first discovered pillar of Ashoka.

The other Orientalists who made up this band of dedicated scholars of Ashoka were men from various fields and countries. One of them was Sir Alexander Cunningham, the same excavator of the Harappan sites. His studies helped establish a chronology for Indian dynasties based on references in Greek and other accounts. Others who were associated with this project were Sir Charles Wilkins, a typographer and Orientalist, who translated the Gita into English. He actively collaborated in the development of the first Bengali typeface, after which printing texts in Bengali took off in a big way.

And so the great mystery of Ashoka's pillars were solved, as scholars from the East and the West worked together like detectives on a case, hunting down antiques, unearthing and decoding old languages, revealing the great story behind the life and times of one of India's most important rulers.

WHO WERE THE KILLER THUGGEES?

A GROUP OF MURDEROUS BANDITS

In the 1830s, a dedicated British official newly posted to the central provinces was shocked to learn about the activities of a group of murderous bandits who operated there. William Sleeman, as he was called, learnt much to his dismay that these were the *thuggees*, who roamed in gangs looting and murdering people, but they were so cunning and deceptive that their victims never knew their true intentions. They always killed by first poisoning their victims, or by attacking them in deserted places, strangling them with a silk handkerchief to ensure a gruesome death.

WHO WERE THESE DREADED THUGGEES?

The earliest mention of the Thuggees appears in a book that talks about the reign of Firoz Shah Tughlaq. This book was written by a contemporary author called Ziauddin Barani who mentions that at some point during the reign of Firoz Shah about one thousand 'thugs' were arrested in Delhi, on the information provided by someone among them. The sultan, with a somewhat misplaced sense of mercy, had refused to execute any of them. Instead he had them shipped off to Lakhnauti or Gaur in Bengal, where they were let loose.

The next mention of thuggees appears during the reign of Akbar (1556- 1605). Many thugs were then arrested and put to death. There were around five hundred of them and came from the Etawah District that lay between the rivers Ganga and Yamuna. This region as well as the province of Agra had always been notorious for the activities of the thuggees.

Shah Jahan offered commissions to thuggees to serve in his army and was thus able to infiltrate their gang. In the year 1666, towards the close of Shah Jahan's reign, the traveller called Jean de Thevenot noted that the road between Delhi and Agra was infested by thuggees. Their methods of killing as described by Thevenot were quite gruesome:

'They use a certain slip with a running-noose, which they can cast with so much slight about a Man's Neck, when they are within reach of him, that they never fail; so that they strangle him in a trice.'

WHAT'S THE STORY BEHIND THEIR ORIGINS?

Well, that's something of a mystery. There's so much myth in the stories about the origin of the thuggees that it's difficult to tell which parts of it are true.

One story goes that in remote ages, a demon infested the earth and devoured human beings as soon as they were created. The world was in danger and the goddess Kali came to the rescue. She attacked the demon, and cut him down; but as every drop of his blood fell to the ground, another demon rose from the drop. And though the goddess continued to slay these new demons, fresh ones rose from their spilled blood as well: they were multiplying as rapidly as they were being mowed down. So finally the goddess decided to change her tactics. So using the perspiration that rained down her arms, she formed two men (yes, sweat-men...ew!) and gave then a handkerchief (rumal) each. She commanded them to put all the demons to death without shedding a drop of blood and her assistants then proceeded to strangle the demons to death.

Once the demons were defeated, Kali was pleased and said that her assistants could keep the handkerchiefs. These men eventually became the thuggees, who used rumals to strangle their victim, just as their ancestors had done many years ago with the demons.

THE MOST DANGEROUS OF THEM ALL: BEHRAM, THE KILLER

THE MOST NOTORIOUS OF THESE THUGGEE WAS A THUG LEADER CALLED BEHRAM, WHO LIVED BETWEEN 1765-1840. HE WAS REPUTED AS ONE OF THE WORLD'S MOST PROLIFIC KILLERS. IT IS SAID THAT HE PROBABLY MURDERED UP TO 931 VICTIMS BY STRANGLING THEM BETWEEN 1790-1840 BEFORE HE WAS HANGED TO DEATH. (THAT'S WAY MORE THAN ANY OTHER SERIAL KILLER IN RECENT HISTORY!)

BEHRAM USED HIS CUMMERBUND (A CLOTH BELT AROUND THE WAIST) AS A RUMAL, OR HANDKERCHIEF, TO EXECUTE HIS KILLINGS. IT HAD A LARGE MEDALLION SEWN ON TO IT. FOR SOME MYSTERIOUS REASON, IT WAS CALLED THE CANOVA MEDALLION. WITH GREAT SKILL, BEHRAM COULD CAST THE RUMAL SO THAT THE MEDALLION LANDED RIGHT AT THE THROAT OF HIS VICTIMS, AND CAUSED A SWIFT AND PAINFUL DEATH.

THE DREADED CANOVA MEDALLION WAS REPUTED TO HAVE BEEN USED IN MANY MURDERS, AND THIS, ALONG WITH AN OLD HAND-WRITTEN DOCUMENT ABOUT BEHRAM'S SON, ARE NOW PRESERVED IN A PRIVATE MUSEUM. BUT IT REMAINS A MYSTERY HOW IT CAME INTO BEHRAM'S POSSESSION. ANTONIO CANOVA WAS A SCULPTOR WHO LIVED IN VENICE AROUND THE SAME TIME. PERHAPS THE MEDALLION THAT BEHRAM HAD RESEMBLED SOMETHING THAT CANOVA HAD CREATED, AND SO IT GOT ITS NAME. BUT THIS MYSTERY HAS NEVER BEEN RESOLVED.

SO WHAT DID THE BRITISH DO ABOUT THESE THUGGEES?

The name 'thug' actually means a 'deceiver'. According to colonial records between 1799 and 1808 the practice of Thuggee reached its height during this time. The British decided that they needed to do something to stop this growing evil. They wanted to show the Indians (the 'natives') that their colonial rule was actually helpful and kind.

In 1810, the bodies of thirty victims were found in wells between the Ganga and the Yamuna, and in 1816, a paper on a tribe of murderers called the *phansigars* (or stranglers) appeared in a scientific magazine. Various officers then made unsystematic efforts to capture these stranglers, but none of those attempts were effective till 1829, when William Sleeman (remember that colonial officer we had mentioned?) finally put a stop to the thuggee menace.

WHOA! HOW DID HE DO IT?

So who exactly was William Sleeman?

In 1809, at the age of twenty-one, William Henry Sleeman was nominated as a cadet in the Bengal army. In 1822, he was put in charge of the District of Narsinghpur, in the Narmada valley. It was here that he first discovered the menace of the thuggees. In every case the modus operandi (a fancy term for method of operation) appeared to be the same.

THE THUGGEES' MODUS OPERANDI

THE THUGGEES WERE MEN WHO WOULD DRESS WELL AND TRAVEL WITH RICH MEN AND KILL THEM ON THEIR WAY. USUALLY THEY BEFRIENDED GROUPS OF TRAVELLERS, OR FOLLOWED THOSE WHO CARRIED TREASURE. THEY AMBUSHED THEM NEAR A DESERTED PLACE AND STRANGLED THEM TO DEATH. THE THUGGEES WERE ALSO PROFESSIONAL POISONERS, A GROUP OF PEOPLE WHO WERE ALSO USEFUL FOR THEY HAD THE KNOWLEDGE OF POISON NOT JUST TO KILL CREATURES SUCH AS SNAKES AND RODENTS BUT ALSO TO HEAL. THE POISON THE THUGGEES USED

MOST OFTEN WAS THE DATURA, A WILD HERB. IT WAS SOMETIMES PUT IN THE HOOKAH TO BE SMOKED, AND SOMETIMES IN THE VICTIM'S FOOD. THE THUGGEES USED ALL KINDS OF DISGUISES TOO.

A POPULAR STORY ABOUT THUGGEES GOES LIKE THIS: A TRAVELLER WHO HAD BEFRIENDED STRANGERS WAS SOON FOUND DEAD IN AN INN. HIS BODY HAD THEN BEEN PLACED IN A LARGE EARTHEN JAR AND ABANDONED.

THE DAROGA (OR POLICE OFFICIAL) INVESTIGATING THE CASE KNEW THE POTTER WHO HAD MADE IT, AND EVENTUALLY FOUND OUT WHICH INN HE HAD SUPPLIED IT TO. THE INNKEEPER CONFESSED THAT HE KNEW OF THE UNLUCKY TRAVELLER AND BUT HE HAD NOT COME FORWARD BECAUSE HE HAD BEEN AFRAID HIS BUSINESS WOULD BE RUINED. BUT HE DID PROVIDE A DETAILED DESCRIPTION OF THE SECOND TRAVELLER, WHO WAS WITH THE MURDERED MAN. HE WAS NONE OTHER THAN ONE OF THE THUGGEES. AND FINALLY HE WAS CAUGHT.

Anyway, around 1830 or so, as the story goes, Sleeman was surprised to learn that a gang of thuggees lived in a village not far from his court house, and that in the extensive groves of Mandesar, quite near his headquarters and now in central India, lay hidden one of the greatest *bhīls*, or places of murder, in all India. In a matter of months, Feringheea, one of the most influential thuggee leaders, was arrested, and his confessions helped Sleeman break the thuggees much faster than he expected.

But Sleeman was now obsessed with the thuggees and putting an end to them. He began seeing thuggees everywhere. In fact, he came to be known as 'Thuggee Sleeman' because he made it the main business of his life to hunt them down. He realized that thuggees were not just limited to his part of the country. There were poisoners all over India, and they were numerous in the Bombay and Madras Presidencies as well as in

Bengal. Sleeman had a tough challenge ahead of him.

In January 1835, Captain Sleeman was appointed General Superintendent of the operations for the suppression of thuggees. In 1835, he began keeping a journal which has later been published as *Rambles and Recollections of an Indian Official*. From 1839 onwards, Sleeman passed most of his time in the North-Western Provinces (as the northwestern part of UP was then called), thoroughly investigating the secret criminal organizations of North India, and hoping to end them once and for all. An old law called the Regulation of 1826 allowed some former thuggees to turn into informants and report on the rest of their gang.

Sleeman also used information from cross-examinations and conversations with thuggees to construct entire family trees depicting the ancestry of the the thuggees. This only confirmed the belief that thuggee was an occupation that was passed on from father to son. Sleeman's cousin Henry Spry even employed phrenology (which we have discussed earlier in the book) to show that thugs were criminals because of their genetic traits which, of course, is a very unscientific conclusion.

During the years 1831-37, nearly 3,266 thuggees were disposed of one way or another. Separate courts were formed at Hyderabad, Mysore, Indore, Lucknow, Gwalior. Thug 'approvers', that is, members of the group willing to give evidence, helped the government to nab their companions. One thug leader called Amir Ali, whose story has been written as fiction was Meadows Taylor in the book *Confessions of a Thug*, admitted his role in the murder of over 700 innocent victims. But instead of being guilty, he expressed his regret that his twelve-year imprisonment sentence had come in the way of his strangling a *thousand* victims!

There were several attempts on Sleeman's life, of course, but he narrowly escaped. On 10 February 1856, while on his way home on board the *Monarch*, Sleeman died near Ceylon.

'Kill him quick!': The thuggees were not known for their kindness

WHAT ELSE DO WE KNOW ABOUT THESE KILLER BANDITS?

Not much. We do know that the British did not coin the word 'thug'. It was in existence in the sixteenth century as *thag* (deceivers/thieves). The term *phansigar* referred to criminals in South India but in the colonial period, the word began to be used interchangeably for the thugees as well.

The thuggees were in no way unique or uncommon in India during those times. There were many other groups like them: the

Pindaris, mercenaries and highway robbers, to say the least. There were also the Gardis who were employed at the same period by the Peshwas. the identities of the thuggees too were quite fluid, they often doubled up as peasants or farmers.

The earliest pieces of information the British collected regarding the thuggees came from Indian landowners and local policemen. The early thuggees were often a kind of 'bandit retainers', who were tied to their patrons by some kind of patron-client relationship. (Think of it as a mini army of killing bandits that were at the beck and call of a rich landowner!)

But the British tended to generalize everything about India, and put them into boxes, so it's now popularly believed that a lot of the thuggee scare of the time was actually constructed by the British. In fact, thuggee became a catch-all phrase used by the British for those who were any kind of outlaws, who were not part of their grand 'civilizing' mission. These included wandering and nomadic groups like the Jats, the Gujjars, the Pathans, the Mewatis, etc., who sometimes plundered and looted settled communities. In the late 1830s, various groups of travelling tribes, like the Sannyasis, Nagas and Yogis, fell victim to this exercise of criminalizing thuggees.

But whatever misrepresentations of the thuggees were done by the British, there is no doubt that for a large part of the nineteenth century, these killer dacoits terrorized all parts of the country, and were some of the worst serial killers known to man.

So the next time you're travelling, don't befriend a mysterious-looking stranger: who knows he could be the last of the thuggees!

WHERE DID NANA SAHIB DISAPPEAR?

A MASSACRE THAT NO ONE WANTED

It was the summer of the year 1857, when across the plains in east India princes, soldiers and even peasants broke out in rebellion against British rule. Near Kanpur, in the fort by the river Ganga, some British families had been taken prisoner. The soldiers who were loyal to Nana Sahib, the adopted son of the Peshwa who had once ruled the Marathas, guarded these prisoners, watching over them night and day as they waited for news of an agreement between their leader Nana Sahib, who was the Peshwa's chosen successor, and the British general. And at last, some news filtered through, it was carried to the soldiers by word of mouth.

The captured Britishers, especially the women and the children, were to be set free. They were to be escorted to the ghats where boats would take them onto Lucknow. But then there was confusion. A fire broke out, some of the boatmen and a few of the prisoners jumped overboard, and then the firing began, indiscriminate and random. It resulted in a massacre, and led to one of the most disastrous events of the revolt of 1857. It was believed that it was the rebel leader Nana Sahib, the man whose right to be Peshwa was disregarded by the British, who was behind it. But then as the revolt was ruthlessly suppressed by the

British, and all the revolt's leaders either died or perished, Nana Sahib alone was never found.

He had disappeared, never to be found again.

WHO WAS NANA SAHIB?

Nana Sahib was one of the leaders of the revolt of 1857 (which you know from your History books). He was born Dhondu Pant, and was the adopted son of Peshwa Baji Rao II, who had been exiled by the British from his kingdom to Bithoor near Kanpur. (Peshwa was a title created by Shivaji for the Maratha Empire; it was a lot like the title of Prime Minister).

Baji Rao II had inherited the peshwaship with help from Nana Phadnavis and Daulat Rao Scindia, two powerful Maratha administrators. But by the time Baji Rao II came to power, the great Maratha Empire had lost much of its glory and there were rivalries between the many groups and factions.

In 1800, Yeshwant Rao Holkar and Scindia, Maratha warlords, marched to Pune, to assert control over the peshwaship. Baji Rao II fled to Bombay and signed a treaty accepting British protection in an attempt to save his peshwaship. But it he still plotted ways to get rid of British control. This ultimately led to the Third Anglo-Maratha War of 1817-1818, which ultimately sealed Baji Rao's fate.

WHAT HAPPENED TO BAJI RAO II?

On November 5, 1817 there was a short war between the British and the Baji Rao II's army. Baji Rao II fled to seek help from the other Maratha chiefs. After running for five months from one fort to another, desperate for help from other Maratha chiefs like the Scindias, the Holkars and the Bhonsles, Baji Rao II finally surrendered to Sir John Malcolm, who was commanding the British forces.

Malcolm allowed Baji Rao II to retain his personal fortune and agreed to pay him a pension of a hundred thousand pounds every year. In return, Baji Rao II would move to a place decided by the

British and never return to his peshwaship. He would have to give up all claims to his throne and could no longer call himself the Peshwa. Baji Rao II, sad and defeated, contented himself with the title of 'Maharaja' and the British did not object to that. Governor General Hastings signed this treaty with Baji Rao II thinking that he would not live very long, he was already above forty and most of his predecessors did not live much beyond that age. (Yes, people died very, very early in those days!)

The British selected a small village on the bank of the Ganga. It was called Bithur, near Kanpur, where there was also a big British military establishment. The place was not very big, but Baji Rao II moved here with his relatives in 1818. Here Baji Rao spent his days devoted to religion and in the company of priests and estrogens of various kinds, for he was a very superstitious man.

BAJI RAO II AND THE GHOST THAT HAUNTED HIM

THERE ARE MANY STORIES ABOUT THE COURT OF BAJI RAO II. ONE OF THEM IS THAT HE WAS FOREVER HAUNTED BY THE GHOST OF NARAYAN RAO, A PREVIOUS PESHWA, WHO HAD BEEN MURDERED. IT WAS A MURDER THAT HAD SUPPOSEDLY BEEN COMMITTED BY BAJI RAO'S FOSTER PARENTS RAGHUNATH RAO AND ANANDI BAI. RAGHUNATH RAO HAD BECOME PESHWA AFTER NARAYAN RAO'S SON, MADHAV RAO, COMMITTED SUICIDE IN 1795. NARAYAN RAO'S GHOST HAUNTED BAJI RAO THROUGHOUT HIS LIFE, AND HE WAS OBSESSED WITH EXORCISING THE GHOST!

EVEN AS PESHWA, BAJI RAO II EMPLOYED THE PRIESTS OF PANDHARPUR, A TEMPLE TOWN OF MAHARASHTRA, TO OFFER PRAYERS AND RITUALS ON HIS BEHALF IN ORDER TO GET RID OF THE GHOST. IN BITHUR, HE PERFORMED RELIGIOUS AMENDS AS RECOMMENDED BY THE PRIESTS OF BENARES. HE ALSO BUILT TEMPLES AND BATHING GHATS, WENT ON SEVERAL FASTS, AND FELL AT THE FEET OF ALL SADHUS AND SOOTHSAYERS.

Contrary to the hopes of the British, Baji Rao II lived for another thirty-three years and died in 1851 at Bithur. Nana Sahib, his adopted son, thus inherited a twisted legacy.

SO WHAT HAPPENED TO NANA SAHIB AFTER BAJI RAO II'S DEATH?

We're coming to that. Nana Sahib was expected to become Peshwa in 1851, but his pension was abruptly stopped because of a new policy called the Doctrine of Lapse. This was devised by Lord Dalhousie. Under this policy, the East India Company took over all territories where the heir to the throne was not the 'natural' (that is, biological) heir, or if the heir was not good enough (to be decided, very conveniently, by the British themselves!). Of course, it was a ridiculous policy, and it was devised by the British to take over as many Indian territories as possible.

This angered Nana Sahib and he threw in his lot with others who were rebelling against the British rule in other parts of the country. This ultimately led to the Revolt of 1857.

WHY DID THE REVOLT HAPPEN EXACTLY?

There are many reasons why the revolt happened. Some of these reasons are so well known that they've become legends (and we're sure you've read all about them in your History books). But to give you a quick recap:

Firstly, the soldiers were scared of using the new rifles the British had introduced. To load it, they were required to bite off the paper cover, which was supposedly greased with beef and pork fat. Both Hindu and Muslim soldiers refused to touch them and soldiers in Meerut, Delhi, Central India, UP and Bihar rebelled.

Plus the soldiers, who were the main rebels, were poorly paid and made to serve in distant lands. Land revenue settlements introduced over the years were very unfair.

There was also a lot of anger at how rulers of the small independent provinces were being treated by the British, who were systematically taking over areas like Nagpur, Sambalpur and Avadh.

The case of the disappearing prince: Nana Sahib

WHAT WAS NANA SAHIB'S ROLE IN THE REVOLT?

There is still a lot of confusion about the role of Nana Sahib in the revolt. It's not clear if Nana Sahib actually led the revolt in Kanpur or simply took part in it. He had already been unsuccessful in claiming his peshwaship. And he was very, very angry with the British. As reports and activities of the sepoys revolting in other parts of the country came to Nana, he gained confidence.

The collector (that is, the head of administration) of Kanpur, where Nana Sahib lived, had promised the British to protect it with 1500 men if the rebellion spread there. Cawnpore, as it was called then, was a British military town, which had developed in the course of the British campaign against Avadh.

When the rebel soldiers reached Kanpur, Nana Sahib persuaded them to fight for him. The British were taken off guard. They had only a few men, and soon they were short of supplies. For days, Hugh Massey Wheeler, the commander of the British troops in Cawnpore held out, but no reinforcements came. In the meantime, Nana Sahib offered the Britishers a safe passage, in return for their surrender, so they could leave by the boats that would take them downstream the Ganga.

THE HORRID MASSACRE AT SATICHAURA GHAT

THE RIVER GANGA WAS UNUSUALLY DRY AT THE SATICHAURA GHAT, AND THE BRITISH FOUND IT DIFFICULT TO PUSH THE BOATS INTO DEEPER WATERS. WHEELER AND HIS PARTY WERE THE FIRST TO GET ON BOARD AND THEY MANAGED TO SET THEIR BOAT ADRIFT. THERE WAS SOON SOME CONFUSION, HOWEVER, BECAUSE THE LOCAL BOATMEN JUMPED OVERBOARD AND STARTED SWIMMING TOWARDS THE SHORE. AS CHAOS UNFOLDED, SOME OF THE FIRE STOVES WERE KNOCKED OFF, SETTING A FEW OF THE BOATS ON FIRE. SOON FIRING BROKE OUT, AND MOST OF THE DEPARTING BRITISHERS, WHO WERE PROMISED A SAFE PASSAGE, WERE IN FACT CAPTURED AND KILLED.

THERE IS A LOT OF CONTROVERSY ABOUT WHAT EXACTLY HAPPENED AT THE SATICHAURA GHAT. NO ONE IS SURE WHO FIRED THE FIRST SHOT THAT DAY. SOME OF THE EAST INDIA COMPANY OFFICERS LATER CLAIMED THAT NANA SAHIB HAD DELIBERATELY PLACED THE BOATS AS HIGH ON THE MUD BANKS AS POSSIBLE TO DELAY THE BRITISH DEPARTURE, FOR THIS MADE THE GROUND UNDER THEIR FEET SLIPPERY AND UNPREDICTABLE. THEY ALSO ACCUSED HIM OF ARRANGING FOR THE REBELS TO FIRE ON AND KILL ALL THE BRITISH AS THEY LEFT.

THE EAST INDIA COMPANY ACCUSED NANA SAHIB OF BETRAYAL AND MURDER, BUT NO CONCLUSIVE EVIDENCE HAS EVER BEEN FOUND TO PROVE THAT THERE INDEED WAS A CONSPIRACY ON NANA SAHIB'S PART.

There was a second, even more horrific massacre soon afterwards. The women and children who had survived the Satichaura Ghat massacre, were taken prisoner and kept at Bibighar (literally meaning 'House of the Ladies'), a villa in Cawnpore, under the care of a tawaif called Hussaini Begum. Nana Saheb wanted to use them as a tool to bargain with the Britishers, who were now approaching Cawnpore, under the leadership of General Henry Havelock. There were reports of massacres of villages by the British armies as they approached Cawnpore and this led many of Nana Sahib's associates to swear revenge on the British prisoners. They opened fire on the women and children inside Bibighar through windows that had been boarded up and ruthlessly murdered them.

Again, there is a lot of mystery about what exactly happened at Bibighar and who gave the order to shoot at the British prisoners. Many say that Nana Sahib was against it, but his associates were too angry with the British to care.

WHATEVER HAPPENED TO NANA SAHIB?

When the British soldiers reached the scene, Nana Sahib had already fled. His associates suffered defeats at Gwalior. the British successfully recaptured Cawnpore and burnt down Bithur, including the residence of Baji Rao II.

But nothing more has ever been known of Nana Sahib. Several authors have written about his disappearance and possible whereabouts. According to the writer Perceval Landon, he hid in Nepal where the ruler, Jung Bahadur Rana, granted him protection. His family also received protection in Dhangara, eastern Nepal, in exchange for precious family jewels.

The British, too, could never trace Nana Sahib. Till the late 1880s, there were rumours and reports that he had been captured and a number of individuals turned themselves in to the British claiming to be the aging Nana Sahib! All these reports turned out to be false, and soon all further attempts to capture him were stopped.

NANA SAHIB IN LITERATURE!

- THERE ARE SEVERAL BOOKS THAT HAVE BEEN WRITTEN ON NANA SAHIB'S DISAPPEARANCE:
- THE FRENCH WRITER JULES VERNE'S NOVEL *THE END OF NANA SAHIB* (ALSO PUBLISHED UNDER THE NAME *THE STEAM HOUSE*), IS SET IN INDIA TEN YEARS AFTER THE EVENTS OF 1857.
- IN ANOTHER BOOK CALLED *THE DEVIL'S WIND*, AUTHOR MANOHAR MULGAONKAR OFFERS ANOTHER INTERPRETATION OF NANA SAHIB'S LIFE BEFORE, DURING AND AFTER THE MUTINY.
- K.V. BELSARE HAS A BOOK ON A MAHARASHTRIAN SAINT CALLED GONDAVALEKAR MAHARAJ, WHO CLAIMED THAT AFTER HE LOST THE BATTLE WITH THE BRITISH, A VERY SAD NANA SAHIB SOUGHT REFUGE WITH HIM AT NAIMISHA FOREST, NEAR SITAPUR, UTTAR PRADESH. GONDAVALEKAR MAHARAJ ASSURED HIM THAT HE WOULD BE SAFE WITH HIM AND ADVISED HIM TO SPEND HIS LIFE IN MEDITATION AND PRAYER.
- SO WHAT ARE YOU WAITING FOR? GET STARTED ON YOUR READING LIST, AND MAYBE YOU CAN COME UP WITH YOUR OWN THEORY ABOUT HOW AND WHERE NANA SAHIB DISAPPEARED!

WHAT HAPPENED TO THE SECRET STILWELL ROAD?

A FORGOTTEN OLD ROAD

As the Second World War raged throughout the world, a secret road was built in India to make sure that essential supplies from north-east India could be quickly transported into Burma and China. After the war this road has been all but forgotten.

For almost a year, between 1942-43, the Stilwell Road (also called the Ledo Road) served as a vital lifeline linking together soldiers and countries at war. But once peace came, things changed again. There were new governments in place in the countries, borders were redrawn and the road lost its significance. Apart from locals in the area, no one remembers it much–all its grand history and most of its mysteries are now forgotten.

Now as Myanmar, as Burma is now known, opens out to the world, there has been a lot of discussion about whether this old road, named after an American general and forgotten for decades, will now be revived. It runs through India, parts of China and Myanmar, some of it lost in miles of dense forests but its revival will promise a new era of travel and cooperation.

WHAT WAS THIS SECRET ROAD ALL ABOUT?

Wars make for unusual situations. Borders change, people suffer, millions move and decisions get made that wouldn't have happened otherwise.

One of the major fronts of the Second World War was Southeast Asia. Here, the Allied forces of Britain, US and China confronted the Japanese as they slowly advanced across Southeast Asia. So far, the Japanese had met with almost no resistance, on land as well as on sea. The Japanese had already captured the Burma Road in 1942, which had earlier ensured that Allied supplies reach China. What the Allies needed was a quick alternative. So it was in these dense forests that lined India's northeast, across Burma, and into China, that the Allied forces built a road, all in preparation for a battle that would decide the fate of South Asia as well as the rest of the world.

The road that was built came to be called the Stilwell Road after the American general Joseph Stilwell, who coordinated the Allied operations. It ran from Ledo in Assam, India, and led to Kunming in Yunnan province of southwest China, passing through the Burmese towns of Shingbwiyang and Myitkina. Stilwell's idea for the road was not just to supply the Chinese forces with necessary goods but to also ensure that it would play a major role in future battles against the Japanese.

The road was an ambitious project and never quite achieved the high aims Stilwell had for it. When the war ended, the road was lost in the swamps and also forgotten as new border lines were drawn post the war.

WHY WAS THE STILWELL ROAD BUILT?

In the nineteenth century, British railway builders and engineers surveyed the Patkai mountains at the northeastern border between India and Burma. (The name in the local language means 'to cut chicken'!) They stopped at the 1120 metre-high Pangsau Pass, that led from Arunachal Pradesh on to northern Burma and concluded that a road could indeed be built through it.

These plans were resurrected again after a few decades. After the British had been pushed back out of most of Burma by

A secret road through the mountains:
The mystery behind Stilwell Road

the Japanese near the end of the Second World War, building this road became a priority, because the Japanese had blocked off the old Burma Road.

'VINEGAR JOE'

JOSEPH STILWELL WAS AN AMERICAN COMMANDER APPOINTED IN THE CHINA-BURMA-INDIA REGION IN EARLY 1942. HIS SARCASTIC SENSE OF HUMOUR AND NO-NONSENSE ATTITUDE EARNED HIM THE NICKNAME OF VINEGAR JOE. HE ARRIVED IN BURMA JUST AS THE ALLIED FORCES COLLAPSED, UNABLE TO RESIST THE JAPANESE. JAPAN HAD SUCCEEDED IN CUTTING CHINA OFF FROM ALL LAND AND SEA SUPPLY ROUTES.

IN JUNE 1942, STILWELL PERSONALLY LED HIS STAFF OF 117 MEN AND WOMEN OUT OF BURMA INTO ASSAM, MARCHING AT WHAT HIS MEN CALLED THE 'STILWELL STRIDE'–105 PACES PER MINUTE! TWO OF THE MEN ACCOMPANYING STILWELL, HIS AIDE FRANK DORN AND THE WAR CORRESPONDENT, JACK BELDEN, LATER WROTE BOOKS ABOUT THIS WITHDRAWAL.

As the Japanese advanced, the Allied supplies to the Chinese began to be delivered via air over the eastern end of the Himalayas. But this was a risky strategy. To minimize risks, Stilwell proposed the building of the road to ensure supplies and to regain the area lost to the Japanese. According to Stilwell, the road would meet both these objectives.

But there were many others who didn't agree with Stilwell's ideas. Chiang Kai-Shek, the Chinese military leader, was only interested in conserving his troops and the Allied supplies for use against any sudden Japanese attack, as well as against a probable civil war in his own country. Naturally, he didn't encourage Stilwell's idea to attack the Japanese, or to train Chinese forces in ground combat. Chiang was also worried that the new American-led forces would become an independent force outside of his control. Stilwell's hands were tied: he had frequent disagreements not just with his allies, the British and the Chinese, but also his own colleagues in the US army.

One of them was General Claire Lee Chennault, who was commander of the famed 'Flying Tigers' troop. As adviser to the Chinese air forces, Chennault proposed a limited air attack against the Japanese in China. Stilwell, on the other hand, argued for a ground attack, *supported* by an air campaign, and recommended that they set up a large infantry reserve. A new ground supply route from India to China would also allow the Allies to equip and train new Chinese army divisions for use against the Japanese and ensure an early conquest of North Burma. Stilwell also argued that the Ledo Road network would be much better than the risky airlifting of supplies.

HOW EXACTLY WAS THE ROAD BUILT THROUGH THE MOUNTAINS?

Well, it was a *long* process!

In October 1942, construction of the road began at Ledo, a tea plantation town in Assam. This operation was managed by both US and China. By December, the road had reached Lekhapani (also in Assam), a depot for trains coming all the way from Karachi and Calcutta. It then passed through Jagun and Jairampur on the Assam-Arunachal border and Nampong in Arunachal before rising to make a steep hairpin bend through densely forested hills to the Pangsau pass.

It was incredibly difficult to take the road through Pangsau Pass. It was even nicknamed the 'Hell Pass'! It took several weeks to cut the road through the mountains there and by January 1943, the entire Pangsau Pass had been traversed. The Pass was almost 4,500 feet high in certain places and marked by hairpin bends and sheer drops and surrounded on all sides by thick rain forests. So you can imagine how difficult it was to build a road there (and without all of our modern technology, too!).

From the Pass, the road descended to north Burma. It had reached the town of Shingbwiyang in Burma by the end of the year.

THE LAKE OF NO RETURN

SOUTH OF THE PANGSAU PASS IS THE LAKE OF NO RETURN IN BURMA. IT IS BELIEVED THAT THE LAKE'S NAME CAME ABOUT DUE TO THE NUMBER OF ALLIED AIRCRAFT THAT CRASH-LANDED IN IT DURING THE WAR. A SECOND STORY HAS IT THAT A GROUP OF JAPANESE SOLDIERS RETURNING FROM BATTLE LOST THEIR WAY AND ENDED UP AT THE LAKE. THERE, THEY WERE STRICKEN BY MALARIA AND DIED AND SO THE NAME OF THE LAKE WAS GIVEN, BECAUSE THEY NEVER RETURNED. ACCORDING TO A THIRD STORY, SOLDIERS FROM THE US ARMY, WORKING ON THE LEDO ROAD, WERE SENT TO EXAMINE THE LAKE AND GOT TRAPPED IN THE SWAMP AND DENSE UNDERGROWTH OF THE LAKE AND DIED WHILE TRYING TO ESCAPE. YET ANOTHER STORY HAS IT THAT THE RETREATING BRITISH TROOPS IN 1942 GOT LOST IN THE QUICKSAND THERE.

BUT NO ONE IS QUITE SURE HOW THE LAKE GOT ITS NAME.

In October 1943, the road reached Tagap Ga, the northern most point till which the Japanese had captured Burma. Soon, it reached the biggest town in Burma, Shingbwiyang, nearly a year after its construction began. The road had crossed several rivers on the way. Vital supplies could now reach the troops who were fighting off the Japanese army around the towns of Kamaing, Mogaung and Myitkina.

From Shingbwiyang there was already a fair weather road that had been built by the Japanese, and the Stilwell Road followed this. Finally, at the Mong-Yu junction, this new road met the Burma Road. It had spanned ten major rivers and 155 secondary streams on the way.

SO WHAT HAPPENED AFTER THE ROAD WAS BUILT?

It was then that Stilwell thought that the time was ripe for the conquest of Myitkyina, a town that the Japanese held in north Burma. It was also necessary to stop the Japanese troops from advancing into Imphal and Kohima, in India.

The battle of Myitkina involved some heavy guerrilla fighting. (Guerilla fighting, for those of you who aren't sure, is a form of warfare where small groups of non-traditional fighters combat the larger, and more traditional military forces.) It involved the Chinese and Allied forces, and the Chindits, a British India 'Special Force' who were masters of guerrilla fighting.

In March 1944, the Chindits set out from an airstrip in Assam and flew over the mountain ranges separating Indian from Burma, and landed in the jungle 130 miles behind the Japanese front lines. They fought with grim determination against their Japanese opponents, blocked the enemy supply routes and stopped the Japanese troops that were making its way into India via Imphal and Kohima.

Things however became difficult when the monsoons came. The fighting continued in a sea of mud, but the Chindits found themselves short of food and ammunition since because of the heavy cloud cover, air-dropping of supplies was not possible. Soon less than *five per cent* of those who still survived were declared physically fit enough to continue the fight.

The Last Desperate Battle for Myitkyina

In April 1944, Stilwell launched his final attack to capture Myitkyina. He did this with the help of a specialized unit of US troops called Merrill's Marauders (named after their commander Frank Merill), who were masters of jungle warfare.

The Marauders now made a gruelling 65-mile jungle march. But since they had been fighting since February in the jungles of Burma, they were suffering from both war injuries and disease. A particularly horrible problem was the outbreak of amoebic dysentery, which left the Marauders weak and unfit for battle.

But despite everything, on May 17, the remaining Marauders attacked Myitkyina airfield with two Chinese infantry regiments. The airfield was quickly taken, but the town was defended fiercely by the Japanese soldiers. Myitkyina did not fall until three months later in August 1944, after Stilwell sent in thousands of Chinese reinforcements. Only a week after the fall of Myitkyina, the Marauders force, now down to only 130 combat-effective men (out of the original 2,997) was disbanded.

The course of the war was by then already beginning to change. The Allies were steadily gaining the upper hand. The Germans and the Italians, who were fighting in other parts of the world against the Allies, had sustained heavy defeats so every effort by the Allied forces was now concentrated in the southeast. It was then, on October 19 1944, that Stilwell was recalled from his command.

SOME FACTS ABOUT THE ROAD

THE ROAD THAT WAS STILWELL'S AMBITION HAD TAKEN TWO YEARS TO COMPLETE (A SURPRISINGLY SHORT TIME FOR THE AMOUNT OF KILOMETRES IT COVERED!). ITS LENGTH WAS ABOUT 1,736 KILOMETRES, AND OF THIS, AROUND 58 KILOMETRES FELL IN THE INDIAN TERRITORY, 1039 KILOMETRES IN BURMA AND THE REST WAS IN CHINA. THE ROAD WAS BUILT BY 15,000 AMERICAN SOLDIERS (60 PER CENT OF WHOM WERE AFRICAN-AMERICANS) AND 35,000 LOCAL WORKERS AT A COST OF US $ 150 MILLION.

WHAT HAPPENED TO THE ROAD AFTER THE WAR?

At the end of the war, when Japan was defeated and Burma liberated, the road gradually fell into disrepair. The last recorded vehicular journey from Ledo to Myitkyina and beyond (but not to China) was the Oxford-Cambridge Overland Expedition in 1955, where six students from Oxford and Cambridge Universities made a journey from London to Singapore on land, in two Land Rovers! (Yes, really. Look it up if you don't believe us!)

This expedition reported that the bridges had been destroyed in the section between Pangsau Pass and Shingbwiyang in north Burma. (After the war, the Burmese military had waged war on some rebels there.)

So the road was virtually forgotten as countries of the region–Myanmar (Burma), India and China–imposed very strict border controls in the years after the war. But in recent years, there has been a revival of good relations between these countries and the opening up of Myanmar to the world has led to proposals about reviving the old lines of communication, which includes the Ledo/Stilwell road. If the road *is* reconstructed, it would be a godsend for the people of the region and would be valuable in promoting trade between our countries.

Who knows, maybe one day we can actually travel down these historical road, where so many battles were fought and forgotten, and finally get to properly meet our neighbours!

ACKNOWLEDGEMENTS

I remain grateful to all the teachers who taught me history—from school to college and beyond—and to historians and writers of history as well.

This book wouldn't be possible without my two wonderful editors being there, every part of the way—Sudeshna Shome Ghosh and Sohini Pal.